14 Tactics to
Triple Sales

By Barbara Hales, M.D.

ISBN: 1467974986
ISBN-13: 9781467974981

Table of Contents

INTRODUCTION

Congratulations! If you've been mining the Internet, looking for gold on how to turn your good business into a great business, I'm here to tell you that you've just struck the mother lode.

This guide will show you how to **triple sales simply by leveraging an asset you already have:** your customers.

You've made a good choice in purchasing *14 Tactics to Triple Sales.* It's a comprehensive resource for generating profit that you can use today, tomorrow, and for as long as you have your business...which will be a long, long time if you use what you learn.

I believe this book is the **ultimate success tool.**

Perhaps the most important thing about *14 Tactics to Triple Sales* is that it's **100% current.**

This is not an old, dusty private label rights book that was written in the 1930's with a new title slapped on it. Quite the contrary! This booked is rich with

emerging 21st Century sales tactics that rely on new technology and reflect the world as it is today.

Of course, all the **traditional approaches to ramping up sales are also included**, but updated and made <u>current for today's profit-focused business owner.</u>

Achieving success requires thinking outside the box. Resources are often limited and the competition is often better armed than you are. It takes creativity, aggressiveness, and sound strategies to overcome these disadvantages.

Making the most of the customers you already have is vital to your success.

Imagine if you could focus your efforts on cultivating the relationship you have with current customers instead of constantly trying to attract new ones. You would talk to your customers, learn their likes and dislikes, and better understand the problems they struggle to overcome.

By spending more time working with current customers you can become a trusted partner, someone who they turn to in times of need. Because of this you will have a better understanding of the dynamic motivations your customers have. You will be able to respond quickly to an ever-changing market. You will out-maneuver your competition by responding quicker.

This relationship is not something that you have to imagine. You can get to the point where your business will sustain itself and grow because of your current customers. It's easier than you think.

Of course you will always need to attract new customers — that goes without saying. However your current customers can do some of that hard work. Through word-of-mouth marketing and formal referral programs your customers can lend a very powerful hand in attracting new buyers.

It is possible to motivate customers to purchase from you repeatedly. And that's a great way to generate more revenue and drive **profits. Turn one-time customers into repeat customers and watch your business soar.**

This isn't fantasy; it's a fact that's been proven again and again. It's turned failing businesses into successes and created **a whole new class of entrepreneurs:** millionaire marketers.

One of the best known, knowledgeable, and widely respected of those marketers is Ted Nicholas. He generously offered his guidance to me when I wrote this book and I'd like to you to "meet" him.

Shake Hands with Ted Nicholas

If you don't know Ted Nicholas' name, you should. He has appropriately been dubbed the business world's "$6 Billion Dollar Man". Ted's companies and the clients that use his strategies have generated a staggering **$6.3 billion (USD) in sales revenue** (to date)

It's no wonder that Ted is widely recognized as one of the **greatest direct marketing wizards of all time.**

Ted's list of accomplishments is extensive and growing He is internationally revered as one of the greatest living copywriters and is perhaps best known for having earned <u>$24.5 million on the sale of a single book</u> which was primarily sold through direct mail.

In all, Ted is the author of his own library of must-have business books: <u>15 bestsellers</u> in all. He made his mark with **How to Form Your Own Corporation Without A Lawyer For Under $75,** and followed it up with titles including **Magic Words**

That Bring You Riches, Billion Dollar Marketing Secrets, How I Sold $400 Million Dollars Worth of Products and Services, and How To Turn Words Into Money.

Ted was a successful entrepreneur long before he became known as an author, speaker and marketing guru. He **founded 23 companies** of his own beginning at age 21. His first business was a highly successful chain of 30 candy and ice cream parlors.

By the age of 24, he was a millionaire.

Financially secure and with multiple profit streams feeding his bank account, Ted sold his business and 'retired' in 1991. The "experiment" lasted three months. Ted discovered he liked working, especially marketing. It was his passion, even more than playing tennis.

Before the year was out, the 'retiree' had launched a consulting and seminar business. A new chapter in Ted's success story was added.

In his current incarnation as the visionary president of Nicholas Direct, this million-dollar marketer distributes his growing library of information products, all aimed at small business marketing success. They are available at his website: www.tednicholas.com.

He's got a lot to offer, so I encourage you to check things out.

Companies large and small on six continents engage Ted for consulting or copywriting work. He earns fees of up to $15,000 (USD) plus 5% of sales per project...and in most cases, an **equity interest** in the business as well.

Ted also holds seminars in Europe and the US on direct marketing and self-publishing, commanding as much as $7500 per person. Attendees don't complain, though. After all, they walk away with million dollar ideas. When he's not traveling for business, Ted is "at home" in Switzerland and Cyprus where he maintains residences.

Now at the pinnacle of his own success, Ted is the go-to guru for television programs including Good Morning America, Today, and Oprah Winfrey as well as hundreds of radio shows, newspapers and magazines throughout the world. But you know what...

Ted still takes time to help "the little guy." One of Ted's greatest gifts is his ability to replicate success. He's created a unique direct-to-consumer marketing approach, which can be applied to virtually any business, investing $100 million (USD) of his own capital to refine his strategy.

He is passionate about small business success and generous with his knowledge. In fact, **Ted Nicholas has contributed personally to this book.** You'll find **Nicholas Golden Nuggets** penned by Ted, himself, throughout the book. Here's one to get you going...

Pearls & Nuggets

This golden nugget is really platinum. Many business owners think a steady stream of new customers will flood them with profits. That is only partially true. The smarter, easier, more reliable way to profit is by selling more to people who have already bought from you. This "little" strategy has a big payoff: **It costs you 6 to 12 times LESS to sell to your existing customers.** (Think what that could do for your profit margin.)

See what I mean? This is the kind of information that many people spend lifetime learning. But you'll be able to follow in Ted's footsteps, avoiding the missteps that can delay success...sometimes permanently.

You'll find Ted's masterful hand in many of the advertising examples cited in the coming pages. Ted's sales writing is unsurpassed in its ability to **transform interest in desire and desire into demand for a product.**

I promise you; it's like getting personal, hands-on guidance from one of the world's top marketer's practically cost-free! On page after page, you'll find the same successful techniques that are making Ted and his clients very rich indeed.

And now it's *your turn* to join the ranks of his super-successful "students." We'll build from the ground up, so it's only natural that first we build a foundation...

CHAPTER 1

THE FOUNDATION OF SUCCESS IS A TRIPOD

Scratch the surface of any successful business and you'll find that it's built on a firm foundation with three pillars

- An incredible product
- An irresistible offer
- **A cost-effective marketing effort**

Let's talk first about your product.

Launching Pad — Your Incredible, Amazing, Unique Product

You create the thing you're going to sell...an information product, a piece of software, and a patented approach to ridding homes of pests. Whatever. Then, you drum up publicity, garner media attention, and put your sales mechanism in place...possibly with the help of one of Ted Nicholas' books. (They certainly make it easier and more profitable.)

With inquiries already beginning; it's <u>time to launch your product.</u> You only get one shot at glory. Don't waste it.

If you don't make a good first impression with a consumer, you'll never be able to establish the long-term relationship...the "customer for life" relationship...that is the *true* source of business success.

A good rule of thumb to follow is that the level of public excitement that you create for any new launch should correspond to your level of confidence concerning the quality of that product.

Bad quality can't hide in the 21st Century. Consumers are accustomed to using digital tools online to **compare prices, features and reviews** for everything from DVDs and digital cameras to chiropractors and, of course, information products.

If your initial product is less than top notch, the word-of-mouth will spread like wildfire, and your business will go down in flames. And deservedly so, by the way.

I don't usually get on my soapbox, but **on the issue of quality...I'm a fanatic.**

Quality Assurance

What small business owners must keep in mind is that through the "care and feeding" of existing customers, a strong **repeat clientele base** can be built, from which word of mouth advertising can become a very strong marketing tool.

Rather than spending great sums of money on mass media advertising, word-of-mouth advertising proves very effective in that actual consumers can vouch for the quality of the customer experience and will act as a motivated promoter for your business.

You pay nothing for what has evolved into the most important marketing commodity in the age of social marketing: real-people testimonials.
Positive word of mouth occurs spontaneously and naturally when your product or service is of the highest quality. So before you launch a product, you need to test its quality. The most reliable way to test any product is **to try it under realistic conditions**.

That means different things for different people.

For example, software and web designers will often run a so-called "**beta test**" of their almost-finished product, in which users have the opportunity to **try a for-pay service or game for free** on the condition that they report any errors in programming or game play.

These types of tests have two main benefits:

- Create positive publicity for the webs sites that offer them
- Give designers and programmers a chance to anticipate and repair possible errors before a product is launched, creating a more successful launch than would occur without the test

Designers of other types of products can enjoy these same benefits by testing their work in **focus groups** or by testing out the product among company employees.

Without a solid product, no entrepreneur can realistically expect to achieve success. However, without a solid method of introducing this product, no small business owner will ever be able to expect to see his or her product take flight either.

Sometimes, even the "big guys" get it wrong.

After the launch of Microsoft's Windows Vista, users began to complain about the operating system's compatibility issues, which included problems with such common pieces of software as the popular iTunes music service.

The **resulting negative publicity,** fueled largely by technology bloggers, put Microsoft in a terrible public relations situation. That translates into skepti-cal prospects, fewer sales, and lost profits.

You want repeat business. You want your customers to be a **positive reference** for potential customers. Make sure that your product does whatever it takes to meet and *exceed* customer expectations. Doing these things will go a long way towards creating satisfied customers.

A lot of future business can be won by positive referrals, word of mouth, and having a reputation as the "original source" of a great first product. **Create a culture that fosters the creation and nurturing of satisfied customers, and you will be viewed as a winner.**

Launching a disappointing product is a little like being the boy who cried wolf. For a significant period of time, **consumers are likely to remain ambivalent** about any new development that you may produce.

Look…a dip in revenue is generally temporary, but the damage to your company's reputation caused by a bad product will hurt you in your wallet for years to come. It is far better to spend your resources on perfecting your product BEFORE it launches than to try to correct problems (and your tarnished image) afterwards.

When Your First Product Is Free

In many sales situations, you may be giving away your first "product" for free. Let's say you're selling an herbal supplement. You might offer a free report on natural health as a way to capture contact information.

You must make sure that your product is top quality even if you're just giving it away for free. A cheap, shoddy "gift" doesn't have much value and it will reflect badly on you. So badly, in fact, that your prospect will probably decide that doing business with you is a bad idea.

So make sure that your first product, whatever it may be, delivers a quality experience. If you do, your buyers will come back for more.

That's *exactly* what you want. Now let's talk more about what your customer wants.

CHAPTER 2

YOUR IRRESISTIBLE OFFER

As you know only too well, you are not the only one vying for your customers' business. Your competitors are, too, and they're doing everything they can to make *their* offer appealing. So you'll have to go "one better" if you want to compete...and win.

How do you do that? With an irresistible offer. But what do we mean by that?

Pearls & Nuggets

An irresistible offer is crafted so that it appeals to logic *and* emotions. It makes the case for the superior value so effectively that the consumer has virtually no choice but to say, "No one in his or her right mind should say no to this offer. I'd be crazy to pass it up."

Irresistible Copy

An irresistible offer does three important things:

- **Instantly compels your prospect/clients to act** by <u>presenting a solution for their problem</u>
- **Explains what your prospects/clients will "lose" or miss out on** by listing the <u>key benefits your products delivers, not just the features</u>

- **"Forces" your prospect/client to say "yes I want it now"** (not in 5 days time) by <u>creating a sense of urgency</u>

When your product is great and your offer is irresistible, your prospects will ask themselves a series of questions.

- "Should I continue to suffer OR should I act now and solve my problem?"
- "Should I continue to feel ashamed OR should I act now and deal with my problem?"
- "Should I continue to envy other people OR should I act now to get what they have?"
- "Should I continue to think about this OR should I act now and ensure that I don't lose out on a

good deal, something that costs less than its value?"

In a nutshell, these questions all ask the same thing, "Should I act now?" An irresistible offer means the answer is "Yes!"

Here's a good example of an irresistible offer made by an outside catering company serving businesses in London. The irresistible offer was **"A FREE Sandwich Platter**."

Now you may wonder what's so irresistible about a bunch of sandwiches, but think about it. The caterer was targeting the people in local businesses who have a need for outside catering services, so it was a great way for prospects to **sample the goods.**

Second, who would ever turn down a freebie? Especially after hearing "There's no such thing as a free lunch."

And third, they had **nothing to lose by ordering**.
I should point out that before making this offer, the caterer did some projections. The company worked out the **lifetime values vs. cost of client acquisition** and realized they could be even more generous in their freebie offer and still profit handsomely in the end.

It didn't take them long to discover that it would cost them up to 6 to 12 times more time, effort, and money to gain new clients. So they "upped" the irresistible factor on the offer and invited prospects to enjoy **FREE Sandwiches and FREE Hand-Baked Cookies**

The offer was sent as a sales letter to 201 highly targeted companies within a two-mile radius of their offices. The results were spectacular. In the space of two weeks they received 78 orders.

But that was just the beginning. More than 50% of the businesses — 35 in all — now **order at least twice a month** and many of them order every single week — more than once!

From sales of zero one-month to sales of over £3,000 a week in less than 4 months, was the outcome. And all because of an irresistible offer.

Pearls & Nuggets

Always look for ways to add value to your products and services before you consider lowering your prices.

Value is a matter of perception. Value is complex as there are many criteria on which people assess it. These could be: convenience, visual or auditory appeal, risk management, price versus benefits, peer recognition, etc.

As a starter, try these simple strategies to add value to your product.

Irresistible Benefits

Did you buy a car with air conditioning just because it had air conditioning — or because it would keep you cool and comfortable on hot days? Did you buy a minivan simply because it had anti-lock brakes and airbags — or because it was safer for you and your family?

Do see where I'm going with all this?

People perceive value in a product that is **multi-purposed** and delivers many benefits. Unfortunately, when it comes time to sales copy, a vast number of business owners make the same mistake: they focus on the features of their product or service...in other words, what it does, how it operates, or what it looks like._

Good sales copy **doesn't focus on the features of the PRODUCT — it focuses on the USER,** and how he or she will <u>benefit from using the product.</u>

Pearls & Nuggets

A feature is something the product has or does, while a benefit is something it does for you.   A FEATURE is one of the components or functions of your product. A BENEFIT is a way in which your product improves the life of the user.

... In other words, a benefit is an answer to the question, "What's in it for ME?"

Benefits are not "quality and service" or "cheapest." They are the answer to questions like: "Why should I keep reading?" or "How will buying this make MY life better?" Or the #1 question on every consumer's mind:

"What's in it for me?"

People don't want shampoo — they want clean, great-looking hair. So shampoo companies have made their fortunes by stressing how their shampoo solves the problem of unmanageable hair, giving people shiny, healthy-looking locks.

By offering benefits instead of features, you will create a higher perceived value, which will translate into MORE SALES.

... And that's a HUGE benefit for you!

Irresistible Price

Consumers, like companies, have their eye of the bottom line. That makes the right price a key element in your irresistible offer. So let's take a moment and look at the <u>four main pricing policies/strategies.</u>

- **Premium Pricing** – Used when <u>a product is considered unique</u> and where a <u>substantial competitive advantage</u> exists. Premium pricing is associated with luxury brands like Louis Vuitton, Jaguar, and Rolex

- **Price Skimming** – In this instance, a high price is set because you have a substantial competitive advantage, but know that the advantage is not sustainable. The high price tends to attract new competitors into the market, and the price inevitably falls due to increased supply. Watchmakers who created digital timepieces and offered the unique product at a premium price employed this technique in the 1970's. As other digital manufacturers entered the market, other marketing strategies and pricing approaches were implemented to keep the original watches competitive

- **Penetration Pricing** — Charged for products and services is <u>set artificially low in order to gain market share</u>. Once this is achieved, the price is increased. This approach was used by France Telecom and Sky TV

- **Economy Pricing** — This is a <u>no-frills low price</u>. The cost of marketing and manufacture are kept at a minimum. Supermarkets often have economy brands for soups, spaghetti, etc

---

Pearls & Nuggets

In the minds of some consumers "Quality costs." Considering selling your product or service at a *higher* price than your competitors. People usually associate higher-priced product with better quality.

Those are the "big four," but there are other important approaches to pricing that can be very helpful in developing an irresistible price:

- **Psychological Pricing** — This approach is used when the marketer wants the consumer to <u>respond on an emotional, rather than rational basis</u>. A wonderful example of this is demonstrated in the consumer's response to 99 cents versus one dollar. Although only a penny separates the price points, the psychological impact is huge

- **Product Line Pricing** — Where there is a range of product or services, a scale of prices reflects the scale of benefits offered by the products. For example, a car wash service could offer a basic wash for 10 Euros, a wash and wax for 15, and a deluxe package with wash, wax, and super-buffering for 20 Euros

- **Optional Product Pricing** — Companies will attempt to increase the amount customers spend once they start to buy. Optional "extras" increase the overall price of the product or service. For example, airlines will charge for optional extras such as guaranteeing a window seat or reserving a row of seats next to each other

- **Captive Product Pricing** — Where products have complements, companies will charge a premium price where the consumer is captured. For example a razor manufacturer will charge a low price and recoup its margin (and more) from the sale of the only design of blades which fit the razor

- **Product Bundle Pricing** — Here sellers com-bine several products in the same package. This also serves to move old stock. Videos and CDs are often sold using the bundle approach

- **Promotional Pricing** — Pricing to promote a product is a very common application. There are many examples of promotional pricing including approaches such as BOGOF (Buy One Get One Free)

- **Geographical Pricing** — Geographical pricing is evident where there are <u>variations in price in different parts of the world</u>. One example of this would be where shipping costs increase price

- **Value Pricing** — This approach is used where <u>external factors</u> such as recession or increased competition force companies to provide "value" products and services to retain sales, e.g. value meals at McDonalds

I Got It for Less

Through the years, master marketers and copywriters have compiled lists of words that capture the eyes and minds of consumers. Two of my personal favorites are Ted Nicholas' *Magic Words that Bring You Riches* and *Magic Transitions – 97 Magic Phrases that Almost Compel Readership.*

At the top of everyone's lists, you'll find:

- **Bargain**
- **Discount**
- **Reduced Price**
- **Special Rate**

There's a common thread in these words and phrases. Each suggests that the price you pay today is less than you'll pay tomorrow. This **increases the perceived value of the offer,** making the consumer <u>more likely to act.</u>

It also suggests that it is a **limited time situation**, making the consumer <u>more likely to act immediately.</u>

This technique is used with great success on the Internet to promote new-to-market information products, supplements, and almost anything else you can image.

Irresistible Bonuses

We make buying decisions primarily based on emotions. However, being rational, thinking and logical humans, we also must justify our decision to buy. We do that by convincing ourselves there is enough value to justify our emotional decision.

So since the beginning of time, bonuses have been used by advertisers to make a buying decision seem logical by **adding so much value to an offer that it becomes irresistible.**

When the benefits of a product are clear and a prospect is becoming emotionally "attached" to the idea of a purchase, he/she will check the price. If that price is somewhat higher than imagined, it is not necessarily a deal-breaker.

Confronted with a high price, a prospective buyer will generally **attempt a value calculation** by figuring out what they are getting for their money. This is where your bonuses come in.

Pearls & Nuggets

Bonuses that are different, relevant and of high perceived value will often **double or even triple online marketing business sales,** and they do very well for offline businesses, too

It's important when promoting your bonuses that you **list their prices – (i.e: "A $45 value" or "Normally $19.95" or "Cover price $16")** so that your visitors are even more compelled to take advantage of your great value-added bargain.

Here are a few ideas for bonuses you can create or find:

- Info-products — create them or buy rights to them

- Free consultation

- CDs, mp3 files, audiotapes — record a book or special report, you've got an audio recording to throw in!

- Software — simple tools to add functionality to the things they buy

- Checklists — so buyers know what to do

- Training programs — to show customers how to use their purchase better

- Discount coupons on future orders

The important thing is to make sure that the value-added bonuses that you offer have **value to the prospect you've targeted.**

Pearls & Nuggets

Don't overdo it on the bonuses. If your product is selling for fifty dollars, don't have two-thousand dollars worth of bonuses or your offer will be to unbelievable for most people. Remember, you can have too much of a good thing sometimes.

Irresistible Guarantee

No one wants to get "burned", and the fear of being "had" is probably the biggest obstacle a consumer needs to overcome before he or she is willing to make a purchase. You can help a prospect hurdle that obstacle with a little "risk management" in the form of a strong guarantee of satisfaction in your sales message.

Pearls & Nuggets

Without a doubt, a few unscrupulous types may capitalize on your guarantee. After one of my clients created the "Boost Business with Blogs" eBook, she reported it was not unusual to see a person purchase it, download it, and request a refund two minutes later. Obviously they hadn't yet read the book, and it was clear that they had placed an order knowing they could get it for free. Still, in my experience, the amount of sales you GAIN from offering a guarantee **dramatically outweighs the risk.**

Strong guarantee wording such as "100% satisfaction guarantee" and "If you're not satisfied, we don't want you money" eliminates the risk of potential psychological stress caused by post-purchase remorse or dissatisfaction.

Obviously the wording will depend on your type of business, but it is essential to include the following:

- **Always put in a time limit**: Your time limit will depend on the shelf life of what you're offering — but make it a decent one. Twelve months is likely to give the customer more peace of mind than 10 days

- **State how quickly you will deal with the problem**: The customer will take your guarantee more seriously if you state how quickly you will deal with a problem. For example — we promise to go back out to a customer on the day they call

- **Put limits on the guarantee**: State that the customer needs to call you as soon as they realize there is a problem and also, that they will not allow anyone else to fix the problem first. This part is extremely important, as a third party could cause far more damage and you don't want to be compensating for this

---

Pearls & Nuggets

The most common time limits are 30 days, 60 days, 90 days, a year, and a lifetime. Some studies show the longer the guarantee, the less returns you'll get. Why? Buyers will often return a product if due to their schedule or other reason they haven't yet had a chance to even try it out.

In general, there are three main types of guarantee

- **Money-Back Guarantee** — If a product doesn't work or the customer isn't satisfied the way it works, he/she gets a refund (which may or may not include ancillary costs like shipping and handling)

- **Satisfaction Guarantee** — Similar to a money-back guarantee, but used more often for services as opposed to products

- **Price-Protection Guarantee** — This can mean either locking in a price forever, such as with services that are billed on a recurring basis, or guaranteeing that you have the lowest price anywhere for that particular service or product

- **On-Time Guarantee** — If your clients are always concerned about getting your service or product on time, this is a good one for you

One question that many business owners ask themselves about their guarantee is, "Should I make it easy or hard to request a refund?" Some business owners make their customers jump through hoops to get their money back. While I understand not wanting to make it TOO easy to get an instant refund, there are risks. If you make it really hard, your customers may just skip dealing with you and go direct to their credit card company.

Pearls & Nuggets

This process is called a "chargeback", which can reflect negatively on the vendor's merchant account standing as well as result in **penalty fees** for the vendor. So obviously, as a vendor, you want to avoid charge backs by making the refund process easy for your customers.

Need some inspiration? Here are **10 irresistible guarantees** you can model your own on:

- SEND NO MONEY NOW. If at the end of 14 days you decide not to keep the book, simply return it without obligation

- If you decide to cancel your attendance any time up to 2:00 p.m. on Day 2 of the live event (which, quite frankly, is highly unlikely), I want you to keep the ($$$$$ value – product name) as my gift for signing up in the first place. (Abraham Publishing)

- We guarantee to have your guttering delivered within 48 hours. If we fail, it's yours FREE

- If you decide to keep the (product name), you can pay for it in a few easy installments. If not, send it back at our expense, and you'll owe nothing. Either way, I'd like to send you a free gift for giving it a try

- Your Money Back! In the unlikely event that our parts or labor fail in any way during the warranty period, we'll pay the cost of repairs plus double that amount for inconveniencing you

- If you don't get all the benefits I have promised and more, simply return the (product name) and receive every penny back—including shipping. I'll pay for the return postage as well! The way I figure it is this: If you're not satisfied, that's my fault, not yours! Why should you have to pay anything for it? You have absolutely no risk whatsoever!

- Try it for a full 6 months. If it doesn't do everything you hoped, simply request a full refund and the $120 in bonuses are yours to keep...

- You'll get everything you see listed here, totally risk free! What do I mean by risk free? Simply this: If our product isn't everything I said it was and more, simply return it for a complete refund including shipping!

- And, as is the policy of all the products we sell in our company, my book and software carry an unconditional, money-back guarantee. If my book and software are not everything that I have said they are and you are not in fact overly satisfied, you will receive every cent of your money back. No questions asked. Since we have been in business for 25 years and we are one of the largest companies in the nation, you can count on that guarantee. (Suarez Corporation Industries)

- Subscribe today. If you think your first issue—or any issue ever—doesn't deliver at least $XXX worth of ideas and information, you can tell us to take a hike. We will cancel your subscription and send a prompt refund for all un-mailed issues, no questions asked. We won't be happy to know that we failed your value test, but that will be our problem, not yours. (Selling Power)

Guarantees are good for your customer, but they're also good for you. First an irresistible guarantee will help you **close more sales.** A customer's fears are quieted when they know that if something goes wrong within the time limit of the guarantee, you will put it right.

They feel safer buying from you because <u>you stand behind your product.</u>

Guarantees help you in another way. Since you have guaranteed to resolve the problem if the customer is unhappy, **they can't demand a refund, or refuse to pay altogether** without first giving you the opportunity to put things right.

When Guarantees Kill

Just as a great guarantee can motivate, so, too, can a guarantee full of "weasel words", only in the opposite manner. Here's a sample of one I read recently:

> "You'll be 100% CONVINCED that the new Widget Business Builder will dramatically increase responses and revenue for your company, or we'll cheerfully refund your money in full!"

Now wait a second! The product isn't guaranteed. My satisfaction isn't guaranteed. The only thing that's guaranteed is that I'll be "convinced" that the product will increase calls and revenues? What does that mean exactly?

Personally, the only way I'm going to be convinced that my ad WILL generate more calls is when I hear the phone ring. The only way I'm going to be convinced that I WILL get more revenue is to see the bank statement with that money already deposited. But this offer doesn't guarantee any of that.

Pearls & Nuggets

A guarantee that has precise conditions you must follow or sneaky wording to qualify will **trigger a red flag** in people's minds. This warning might only be subconscious, but the customer will feel the need to take some time to consider your offer...and probably reject it.

Other Irresistibles

Want to drive prospects wild with desire? Show them how to achieve a "net zero" expense when they purchase your product. Include a **referral rewards program** or **affiliate opportunity** in your sales message.

Online affiliate programs are extremely common, possibly because tracking software and other technology have made it so easy to create and run them. Information product publishers don't even have to set up their own processes. Companies like ClickBank do all the work.

Pearls & Nuggets

Affiliates make an outstanding sales force for any product or service. Generally satisfied customers themselves, they provide sincere, positive word of mouth for your business and hopefully a steady stream of prospects. And unlike a traditional sales force, affiliates don't need an office, don't take vacations or sick days, and usually don't ask for a raise!

Another irresistible element that you can add is a **third-party endorsement.** Testimonials from satisfied customers are compelling and reduce skepticism but a thumbs-up from an established expert or beloved celebrity is even more effective.

A product endorsement is a form of testimonial from someone, which indicates that they like or approve of a product. Commonly, product endorsements are solicited from people who are **socially prominent**, allowing companies to advertise their products with statements like "as used by such-and-such an actress," or "the official product of company/event X." It's hard to miss a product endorsement on product packaging and in advertisements; most companies keep their endorsements front and center so that they are always in the public eye.

The concept of the product endorsement is quite ancient. In England, for example, several companies have been advertising themselves as "by appointment to the Queen" for hundreds of years, indicating that they enjoy the patronage of the British royal family.

Pearls & Nuggets

Consumers are often attracted by the idea of purchasing a product, which is endorsed by someone wealthy or famous, as though by buying the product, **the consumer also becomes affiliated with the person who endorses it.**

You can also refer to business alliances you've formed with other respected companies. And you may even want to include a reference to your membership in **professional organizations**. These affiliations **increase your credibility.**

At the heart of an irresistible offer is a prospect's perception that he/she will not be disappointed. One of the best ways to foster than perception is with an offer of **after-sales service.** It provides a "guarantee of satisfaction" like nothing else.

After-sales service can take many forms, from an online database of frequently asked questions to a live help line that's manned 24 hours a day. Interestingly, including a comprehensive list of contact information in a sales message goes a long way in assuring customers that their needs will continue to be met by a business.

Contact information says, "We're committed to your ongoing satisfaction. And unlike a fly-by-night operation, when you need us, you can find us."

To sum things up, **logic and emotion both play a role in consumer buying decisions.** Consumers who perceive that a product has a superior value then have a logical reason to make a purchase. But superior value also presses a consumer's psychological "hot buttons" that are tied to emotions like greed.

Your goal with an irresistible offer is simple. When customers evaluate competing products, they'll discover that **you offer more VALUE.**

Your Ongoing Marketing Campaign

You've got a great product and an irresistible offer. Is that enough? No.

It would be nice if having a great product were enough to succeed. You could sit under a coconut tree; your product by your side, and people would come from miles around just to buy from you.

In the Hollywood movie *Field of Dreams*, Kevin Costner is told, "If you build it, they will come." It doesn't work like that in real life...at least not very often. It you want people to buy your product or service, you have to spread the word.

One notable exception to this hard and fast rule: "Hello Kitty."

Hello Kitty, Good-bye Marketing

This marketing phenomenon from the Japanese company Sanrio, made her debut Nov. 1, 1974. She has a net worth in the billions, UNICEF has given her a special honorary title, and she has her own theme park in Japan and her image graces thousands of products, from 50-cent stickers to expensive jeweled purses.

> Unlike a wide range of children's toys from Barbie to Mickey Mouse, Hello Kitty has relied solely on her charms to build herself into the global phenomenon she is today. Yet, she has never been marketed to consumers!

If you're convinced that you're Sanrio and have created the next Hello Kitty, then good for you. Your product will sell itself now and for years to come. Congratulations. You don't need this book.

But...if you're not Sanrio and your product needs more help than Hello Kitty, there are proven business theories and practical business strategies we can use to consistently drive sales.

So let's talk about marketing...and Ted Nicholas' "The Ice Cream Cone Theory."

CHAPTER 3

THE ICE CREAM CONE THEORY

This chapter is designed just for you. It's aimed at an entrepreneur who truly wants to build an extremely profitable company. A business, which remains successful forever.

To succeed in a big way, of course, you must attract first-time customers. This requires a saleable product. But rarely can a single product sustain an entire business for long. You must also have follow-up products resulting in *repeat business.* Direct marketing jargon for this is a good "back end." Why?

It's nearly impossible to survive and prosper with a single product, with one exception. You market a product, which requires renewal or replacement. It's well known on Wall Street that one-product companies have the highest mortality rate.

Therefore, *before* you begin marketing any product or service, have your back end in place.

Do not make this common mistake. Start out with one product. Get some sales. Realize you need more sales. Then frantically search for other products to sell your customers. You will lose valuable time and sales, which can never be replaced.

To attain a successful outcome, first you must think through the desired result.

Therefore, here is how I recommend you think about your business. Create a mental picture of an ice cream cone! I call it the "ice cream cone theory."

Regardless of the kind of business in which you are engaged, the principle I'm about to discuss applies.

To make this clear, let's look at a hypothetical situation. Let's say you are in information marketer of products directed to the niche market of CPA's and accountants. Here is what your cone might look like:

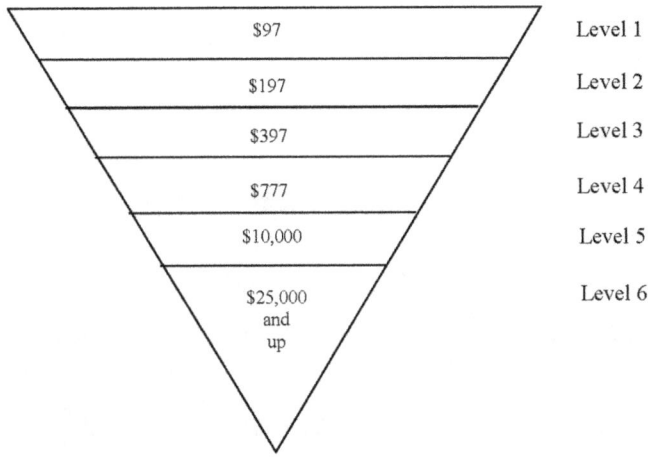

$97	Level 1
$197	Level 2
$397	Level 3
$777	Level 4
$10,000	Level 5
$25,000 and up	Level 6

Products in our ice-cream cone could be as follows.

Level #1. A special report entitled, "7 Secret Ways to Legally Cut Small Business Owners' Taxes to Practically Nothing."

Notice your cone is widest at the top. You want to capture as many people as you can at this stage.

Clearly your first product is the most important. Otherwise, you won't get a second chance to make a first impression. So your goal should be to **astonish the customer!**

Make sure your product quality and packaging are more than what the customer expected. Then your customers will be very receptive to other offers. Why? Because trust has been established by how satisfied the customer is with the product and service. Trust is the key to any long relationship which can last a lifetime.

Pearls & Nuggets

Stay within your niche. Do not make the common mistake of entering an entirely new market.

Level #2. This product is a 6-cassette audio album of a one-day seminar on exactly the *same* subject as the book, "7 Secret Ways to Legally Cut Small Business Owners' Taxes to Practically Nothing!"

Level #3. This product is a two-video package, which captures a live presentation on "Tax Saving Secrets You Should Reveal to Clients Without Being Asked."

Level #4. This product is a 2-day seminar "boot-camp" entitled "Secrets of Maximizing Profits From Entrepreneur Clients." (Notice all products are clearly related.)

Level #5. This product could be any one of the following:

- A day of consultation

- An advanced 3-day seminar on "Getting Rich With Your Accounting Practice"

- Daily rate for services as an expert witness in tax cases

Level #6. This is a minimum annual rate retainer for a growing small company, or monthly billings to a public company in need of extensive services.

The Ice Cream Cone Theory depicts a client "metamorphosis" that includes these stages:

- **Prospects** — At this stage people may not even have heard of you so the aim is to seek new customers. Consider encouraging potential customers to try your products or services, perhaps for free or at a discount

- **Customer** — The Prospect has now moved from trying your product to purchasing from you, but only once. It's very early days in the relationship and you need to make sure they are happy with what they've purchased

- **Clients** — These are customers who make multiple purchases. Now you have them. Now it's time to think about implementing a "loyalty program". Remind them of the benefits of your company and products, always encouraging them to buy more from you. The more they buy, the more loyal they become. If you forget about your clients, they will quickly forget about you. So keep in touch regularly (AT LEAST ONCE A MONTH)

- **Supporter** — At this stage they like and trust you. They believe you have their interests at heart and look after their needs. They're still vulnerable though. If a competitor comes along with a better offer or you fail to deliver they may consider using someone else. You need to maintain the loyalty activities

  Think of a Supporter as someone who would recommend you to a friend or colleague if asked for a good supplier of your product or service. They are good targets for referral programs

- **Advocates** — Customers at this stage are likely to promote your company without being asked first. They depend on you for a particular aspect of their lives or business and wouldn't want to lose you. Make sure you spend time with them as it would make a noticeable impact on your bottom line if they were lost

  They would also welcome the opportunity to help you develop your business as it makes them realize that you value, respect and appreciate them. Invite them to regular forums to discuss new initiatives and perhaps even to the office Christmas party.

You will have very few Advocates, but slightly more Supporters. The longer you've been in business the more you'll have. Most of your purchasers will be at the Customer or Client stage.

At least until you finish this manual and learn how to turn your customers into raving fans.

The key is that you should definitely devote time and attention to Customers and Clients, since they are more likely to buy than your Prospects are. Of course you can't neglect Prospects as you need a regular flow of new customers, but they are a harder sale.

That's why you should definitely **focus your resources on where you are likely to get the greatest return**s, i.e. Customers and Clients.

I love this graphic illustration because it makes it so clear how to **step up the price points** of your new products. And how to think about your business effectively. Most importantly, it dramatically portrays that **the majority of your business profits come from the smallest group of existing custome**rs.

Ted's sales funnel starts at the top with a **high-value, low-cost product**, with a price point of under $100. It's targeted at prospects that don't know him and don't want to risk a lot to see if his product delivers everything he promises.

At the next level is an **enhanced version of the core product**. In this example, it's a set of audio-cassettes of the eBook. This sale is targeted at a smaller group of prospects...Ted's existing, satisfied customers.

The third level is an even more comprehensive package. This home study course Ted offers includes expanded information presented in a range of learning formats. Again, it is for satisfied customers, but an even smaller group..the "select few" who <u>know from previous experience</u> that Ted can take them to the next level.

Ted's reputation becomes more and more solidified with each of the first three product levels. From a broad group of low-paying consumers, he's created a small but lucrative group of customers who are willing to pay $10,000 per person to attend these seminars.

This is also the level at which Ted's limited number of blue-chip clients can be found. These are companies that engage him with $15,000 contracts and a percentage of sales (5%).

Ted's top clients can be found at the bottom of the cone. Already experiencing their own high levels of success thanks to Ted's teachings, these clients these clients pay $100,000 to $200,000 for consulting contracts, offering equity in the company and stock options as part of the deal.

But what does this all mean to you? Let's say you want to **earn $200,000 a year with an information product**. The Ice Cream Cone Theory shows the best way to accomplish that.

If you sell a $100 eBook, you'll need to convert 2,000 people to reach your goal.

But let's say you create an audio version of your product to offer to customers who have mentioned they would love to be able to listen to it. Sell a tape set of your books for $200, and you can cut your sales figure in half to 1,000.

Can you see where I'm going with this? If you create customers for life, people who want to buy from you again and again, you need to sell less to make more.

In business building, it's about the level of your profit, not the number of customers you have. In Ted's cone, all it takes is **one satisfied customer** at the bottom to provide you with your annual income.

It may take time and effort to get that one satisfied customer, but the long term rewards merit the initial investment.

Never forget that it is far less difficult to make one large sale to a customer who already knows you than to make a dozen smaller sales to skeptical prospects who don't yet know from experience that you're honest, trustworthy, and the right person to do business with.

CHAPTER 4

THE ONLY 3 WAYS TO BUILD YOUR BUSINESS

First some clarification to make sure we are all on the same page here. When I use the phrase *grow your* business, I'm referring to **generating more revenue** and, by extension, **increasing your profits**. This guide is not intended to turn you into a multi-national goliath with trillion dollar assets. It's not about the big money game of mergers and acquisitions, leveraged stock buyouts, or anything like that.

This book is about making more money by simply selling more products or services to more people more often. Period.

Okay.   Now that we're clear on that point.   Let's get down to the nitty gritty.

There are three things any business can and must do to be profitable. They are

- Get more new customers
- Sell more to existing customers
- Create customers for life

Each of these pursuits is essential, but one is more profitable. Let's examine all three and see if you can pick the winner.

Business Builder #1 — Get New Customers

Every business inevitably experiences the fact that attracting new customers is an ongoing challenge. Your existing customers know how well you take care of their needs — and they keep coming back to you. But in order to grow, a business needs **a steady stream of new customers.**

Pearls & Nuggets

There are lots of strategies, tactics, and ideas for getting new customers. But this is the most important tip of all: Do *something*...do *anything*...don't wait for business to come to you.

Call it action, call it execution, or call it implementation. Whatever you call the process of turning your business-building ideas into reality, you must commit to that process and **act on your commitment.**

There are two actions you can take to increase the number of customers you have:

- Reach new customers with your existing offering
- Develop a new offering.

Ideally you will leverage the offering you have to enter a new market or expand the reach in your existing market. Five key questions to answer to increase the number of customers are:

- Who has a real need for the product/service I'm selling?
- Does my product meet that need in a manner that either saves money or provides additional value?
- How much, if anything, are they spending to address that need today?
- How many of those potential customers are there?
- How do I reach them?

Capturing New Customers

Without a doubt, **cold calling** is a frequently used, but extremely challenging way to generate business. Cold calls are often perceived as intrusive, and I know very few people who actually enjoy cold calling. However, it can be a good way to uncover qualified prospects in a relatively short period of time.

Pearls & Nuggets

Be sure to start your conversation with a good opening to capture the other person's attention such as "Hi, this is Mary from Widget Firewood. I'd like to talk to you about how to reduce your heating bills by 30% this winter."

Networking is perhaps the most commonly used approach by small business owners. However, it is often poorly executed. Many people attend a networking function and take the wrong approach by trying to meet as many people as they can. They bounce from person to person, handing out business cards like it is an Olympic event and they are vying for the gold medal. They fail to realize that the <u>most effective way to network is to</u> <u>cultivate relationships and give referrals to other members first.</u>

Choosing the target market is probably the most difficult part of attracting the attention of new customers. Once you know who you are targeting you must find a way to attract their attention. This is often done by using **custom promotional products**.

Promotional products are simply items with your company name, logo and basic information printed on them that are gifted to potential clients or existing customers. The items are typically of general interest and are something that will catch the eye of the prospective client. Promotional products can range from pens to golf balls to deluxe engraved crystal. It all depends on your <u>focus, industry and target client.</u>

One of the best ways to attract new customers is to offer **reduced rates or freebies for first-time customers.** Lawyers do it. Pet groomers do it. Even dentists sometimes do it. Your ads or flyers could contain special coupons providing such reductions or freebies for first-time customers.

Sometimes **newspapers have special coupons pages** that group together numerous discount offers from local retail businesses and professionals. By placing your coupon in this particular section, you may experience a <u>greater return on your advertising dollar</u> because it's likely that the group of coupons will attract the attention of readers more than a single, isolated coupon would.

Pearls & Nuggets

Even if you get no response the first few times your coupon appears, people will remember seeing the coupon and will look for it when they need the service or product you provide. Note: always have your logo on the coupon, along with your business name and phone number.

Consider **setting up a contest**. The winner receives a month of free service, or a specific amount of free product. The key to a successful contest is to advertise it as widely as possible. To cut down your advertising costs, try to make the contest exciting and interesting enough that it will be covered by the local media.

Drawings for prizes are another way to bring in new customers. The key to a successful drawing is to give away enough of your service or product that people are really interested in entering.

Using blogs to attract new customers

Social media marketing is quickly replacing traditional online marketing as the go-to technique to reach new consumers. Business owners are turning to alternative techniques, such as **blogs, podcasts**

and RSS feeds to get the word out and the customers in.

To be successful, social media marketing must have **content that is current, topical, and applicable to the social community where the post appears.**

The Downside of New Customers

Is there a down side to focusing on new customers as your profit source? There is, indeed. Marketing requires resources (time, effort, energy, and money.) When aimed at gaining new customers, it **requires much more in resources to accomplish significant results.**

Marketing for new customers is usually NOT the most cost-effective way to generate new revenue both short term and long term. Think of it like this: How much do you currently spend on marketing to attract new customers?

If your marketing budget was $2,000 a month and on average it brought in 20 customers who spent on average $200 each, you are essentially spending $2,000 to bring in $4,000 resulting in a net of $2,000. Of course, for retail business and product sellers, their profits margins may make this even less attractive. However, what would it take for you to bring in 20 new orders a month to an already existing customer base? Maybe if you sent out a mailing costing about 50 cents each to 300 old customers, 20 would respond. In that case, it cost you only $150 to bring in the same $4,000 in revenue.

That's good business whatever profession you're in.

Business Builder #2 – Sell More To Existing Customers

It's often easier and more effective to sell more to existing customers than it is to acquire new ones. Once you understand *why* your existing customers buy from you, you can examine ways of getting them to buy more or more frequently.

The Pareto principle — often referred to as the 80/20 rule — says that 80% of your success in any given field is often due to 20% of your effort. In the world of marketing, this translates into:

80% of your profits come from
20% of your customers

You can use the idea as a starting point to analyze how you can sell more to existing customers. For example, if a small number of your products and services account for most of your profit, can you sell more of the less profitable products to your customers? Or if your higher-margin products or services are only being sold to a small percentage of your customers, how can you raise that percentage?

Where appropriate, encourage customers to **buy a premium product or service** that better meets their needs and provides a superior return for you. This is known as "trading up".

It's also useful to focus on **selling complementary products**. For example, hairdressing outlets sell hair care products for customers to use in their own homes.

Business Builder #3 – Create Customers for Life

"Once a customer, always a customer!" Wouldn't it be nice if that were always true! But we all know it isn't. Future transactions and referrals have to be fought for almost as hard as the initial transaction.

What transpires during stage two of a transaction – what I refer to as *the reinforcement stage* — determines, to a great degree, whether you will be enjoying a one-time relationship with your customer or whether the customer will become a repeat customer and— even more important— a customer for life who recommends your firm to their friends and associates forever after.

Or perhaps I should say "happily ever after."

The reinforcement stage is especially important to your firm's profitability because, time and time again, it has been proven that repeat customers are less expensive to advertise to and—hence—more profitable to sell.

The generally mentioned statistic is that **it costs 6 to 12 times as much to sell a new customer than an existing one.** This is especially true now with e-mail, since you can advertise to repeat customers without incurring any media, printing, addressing, or postage expenses.

The reinforcement stage is valuable for another reason. It provides you with an opportunity to avoid buyer's remorse, which often leads customers to try to return a previously purchased item. This stage also provides you with opportunities to sell additional products to a customer—enhancing their original purchase.

Finally, marketing to customers during the reinforcement stage makes it easy for you to cultivate word-of-mouth referrals among their friends and coworkers.

The "Prodigal" Customer

A prodigal customer is one who, like the Biblical prodigal son, was lost and is found again. If people have bought from you before, they may buy from you again. You need to find out why they stopped buying from you and apply that knowledge to regain their business.

First, **try and find out what changed**. Identify why customers stopped buying from you. Was your product or service:

- No longer necessary?
- Too expensive?
- Unsatisfactory?
- Beaten by a competitive offer?

Research suggests the reason many customers stop buying is because they don't feel that they have sufficient contact with their suppliers. If you don't have some form of regular contact — e.g. monthly or quarterly phone calls, formal or informal visits to customers, mailshots or email newsletters — customers may feel they are being ignored and look elsewhere.

If you have lost a customer for these reasons, your first step is to **rebuild contact** and prove that you understand and are focused on their needs. One-way to accomplish that is with <u>a letter expressing regret that they have stopped buying</u> from you and making them a time-limited offer.

It's worth trying a few times, but don't keep persisting if you aren't getting any response. Many businesses have a limit to the amount of times they contact lapsed customers — usually five or seven times.

Once you've determined why the customer is no longer buying from you, **consider ways to make your business more appealing.**

For example, if you learn that customers feel your **price** was too high, consider a time-limited discount to encourage them to start buying again: *Come back for more and we'll discount your purchase by 20% for 3 months.*

If your service or product **performance** was rated unsatisfactory, ask what you could do to make it meet your customers' expectations and assess if it is possible and profitable to offer: *Give us another chance and we'll make sure you're satisfied...or we'll return 110% of your purchase price.*

Let Sleeping Dogs Lie

While you may be able to tempt many customers back, remember that you don't want them at all costs. You want to build a long-term profitable relationship with a consumer who is likely to buy from you now or in the future. You don't need to "romance" deadbeats who are only in a relationship with you for the freebies.

The bottom line: it's not usually a good idea to make long-term offers that don't contribute any profit just to get a specific customer back, unless there are compelling strategic reasons to do so.

CHAPTER 5

TURNING GOLD TO PLATINUM

I've never doubted for a minute that The Girl Scouts of America are master marketers. But it's not just the fact that they have a legion of sweet faced girls going door-to-door with an impassioned, personal, emotional hot-button-pushing pitch that I'm talking about.

Actually, it's a lyric in a popular Girl Scout camp-fire song that lets me know they're tuned in to what makes a business thrive:

Make new friends, but keep the old,
one is silver and the other gold.

New customers are great and selling more to existing customers is a golden opportunity that can last a lifetime. That makes nurturing a relationship with existing customers a blue-chip investment that yields platinum-level returns.

Your 5 Goals When "Preaching to the Converted"

There are five basic marketing goals during what I have referred to as the *re-enforcement stage* of a sale. Most involve driving customers back to your Web site to take an action or learn more about the products or services you offer. They get information and savings.

Here's what *you get.*

- **You build strong emotional bonds** with customers by thanking them for their patronage, expressing your appreciation for their purchase

- **You find out more about the customer's needs** and possible ways you can satisfy them—including improving your firm's performance

- **You provide incentives to purchase additional products or services** that complement the customer's original purchase

- **You plant the seed for future purchases and maintain the buyer's enthusiasm** by describing new products and services as they become available

- **You provide customers with the tools they need to become your advocates** and recommend your firm to their friends and coworkers

A few enterprising firms have always done these things. But the problems of maintaining customer records and the costs—primarily printing and postage—associated with customer retention programs worked against their success. With e-mail, however, reinforcement can operate virtually cost free.

All that's needed is the discipline and imagination to set the program in motion and constantly search for new ways to re-approach old customers.

Existing Customers Are Your Most Profitable Resource

Smart marketing is about getting new customers. Triple Your Sales marketing is about **getting, keeping, and re-selling the most profitable customers**. For every important reason, current customers are more important to you than new customers.

Here's why:

- **Current customers are more willing to buy new products** because they already know you. There are studies in many markets that support this position. This helps you <u>save money by working less to make the sale</u>

- **Current customers are the fastest and most reliable source of sales of a new product**. It is surprising how many companies will overlook targeted mailings to their existing customer base, or do not keep sufficient customer records and must buy mail lists for each new product. The ROI (Return on Investment) on direct mailing to existing customers in a well defined database can be outstanding when compared to broad based advertising or purchased mail list to prospects. This helps you <u>generate money easily with one, rather than multiple pitches</u>

- **Current customers are willing to work with you** on structuring their buying patterns so that they buy more economically/cost effectively from you. Existing customers set up auto-billing, standing orders, blanket orders, and this can allow you to approximate buying volume so your company can do better production planning. This saves you money because improved production planning will <u>reduce your cost of sales and increase your profit</u>

- **Current customers provide a ready source of competitive information** and information on potential new products. And unlike a market research firm, your customers don't charge you for the data so you save money

---

Pearls & Nuggets

You will likely offer current customers rewards of some kind for answering questionnaires, providing feedback, etc. But the right rewards, such as discount coupons and other sales-related benefits, will generate profits rather than expense.

CHAPTER 6

THE #1 PROFIT-ROBBING MISTAKE THAT BUSINESS OWNERS MAKE

Most owners and managers want to grow their business. Most of them concentrate exclusively on getting more new customers. Odd really.

There is lots of marketing research that is pretty consistent in pointing out that it costs somewhere between six and twelve times as much to get a new customer as it does to sell to an existing customer.

And once you have a customer it is generally pretty straightforward to get them to buy from you more often.

What's that? Your business is different. You sell a one-off product. There's no way to get customers to buy more often.

Maybe...but I don't think so.

The world is filled with failed business that failed to see that every one-time buyer can be a customer for life. For example, I know of a high-end U.K. business that builds solid wood kitchen units equipped with the best possible kitchen equipment and a "life expectancy" of 20 years or more. The owner told me that he can't use a customer for life.

He's wrong. According to housing statistics, U.K. residents move every 4.7 years on average. When they do, isn't it possible that they'll want to replace the kitchen in the *new* house? So keep in touch. They just might buy from you again.

And what do you know about your customer. Top of the list is that they want to improve their homes and they will pay good money to get top service. They probably are willing to spend money to improve the rest of their home.

Could you do some joint-venture marketing with another, non-competing, home improvement company? Look around. You will find plenty of other companies that would love to be able to market directly to your customers.

Sure, you are not marketing your own service — but does that matter? If you work a deal with another home improvement company they are certain to pay a commission for each of your customers that buy from them.

And finally, let's say you're that rare business where the first time is the only time a customer will ever buy from you. Okay. Your product is truly once-in-a-life-time purchase. But only for that customer. You can leverage your customers' satisfaction into compelling endorsements and testimonials that help you make more sales to strangers, and referrals to make more sales to friends.

Win-win-profit.

Ted Nicholas's Story: I Didn't Realize What I Was Missing (Millions of $)

I discovered I could get customers early on. At the age of seventeen, I was pounding the streets selling Kirby vacuum cleaners door to door. At age 21, (and $96,000 in debt, by the way) I started "Peterson's House Of Fudge."

It was in the sweet business of candy-selling that I began to realize that I could *really* sell.

I grew my business from a single flagship store to 30 retail franchises.

It was around this time that the idea for my first book began to take hold. "How to Form Your Own Corporation Without a Lawyer for Under $50" contained all the necessary tear-out forms to incorporate yourself. (By the way, when I re-issued the book, I had to change it to "How to Form Your Own Corporation Without a Lawyer for Under $75.")

I created the book and the online marketing message that turned it into a best seller. When I wanted to expand my profits, I just wrote another book and another sales letter. I realized I was on to something. And soon my publishing empire —Enterprise Publishing — expanded to include <u>14 other best-selling business books</u>.

From Enterprise I created an incorporating service company called The Company Corporation which has grown to become **the largest incorporating company in the world.**

I was a success, yes, but I was a fool. I was leaving millions of dollars on the table and I didn't realize it. I was so successful at generating *new* business that I had failed to take advantage of the thousands of satisfied customers who were **literally wishing that I would sell them something new.**

This book will help you avoid the mistake I made. It's a mistake that cost me a lot of money before I "got wise" to **the lifetime value of customers.**

If you ask the world's most successful sales people, they'll tell you that finding, and selling to, new customers is actually one of the hardest tasks they have. You have to get the trust of your prospective customer, get onto their level, and do a lot of legwork. You also have to qualify the customer, and see whether they can actually buy your product. It can be a lengthy process!

Of course, **your existing customers are already familiar with you**. You probably don't need to convince them of your reliability. After all, they wouldn't have originally bought from you if they thought you were crazy, would they? You've developed a reputation (hopefully good!) and you can use this to your advantage.

The only thing that could damage your chances of selling to existing customers is when your customers have genuine complaints about your service. If you're not reliable and offer a poor service, then don't rely on being able to sell to existing customers. Of course, most of you treat your customers in high regard; they're the lifeblood of your businesses!

And once you get the lifeblood flowing continuously, your cashflow and profits will surge.

Let's get started!

CHAPTER 7

14 TACTICS FOR INCREASING PROFITS NOW

According to the U.S. Small Business Administration, it's <u>much easier to drum up additional business from previous customers</u> than it is to find new customers. The SBA even goes as far as to say that it's **65% easier to convert a sale** from someone you sold to in the past.

In the next pages, I'll outline a series of practical, affordable, you-don't-have-to-be-a-rocket-scientist techniques that can start adding zeroes to your bottom line in a matter of months, if not weeks. They'll help you deepen your relationship with existing customers and strengthen the ties that bind consumers to your business so that they buy from you again and again, recommend your business to friends, and continue to generate profits.

In order to make your second sale and the ones that come after that, you need to make the first one...and you need to make it right. Your first sale is the foundation that you build on. Don't let it be shaky.

Tactic #1 — Kill Them with Quality

Nothing is more important than the quality of your primary product. It is the centerpiece of your business and how well it delivers on the benefits it promises will determine whether your customers are disappointed, satisfied, or so thrilled that they would buy anything else you have to sell.

How do you define a "quality" product? That's a good question.

A quality product is one that **meets its consumer's needs better than most competitors**. Where the benefits are so blindingly obvious, the prospect sees it and says "That's exactly what I need, it's worth every penny and more, and I've got to have it."

A quality product is sometimes the **"first" to solve a problem**. Or it's a staggering, a quantum leap **improvement over any previous offerings**. Or it's something that's offered at an **affordable price** that was once available only to the very, very rich.

Ted's Story — Adding Value

Personally, I like to "kill" with quality and **combine all of these attributes** into my products. I love being the first author to tackle a subject such as self-incorporation without legal fees.

My approach is to astound my customers with **more value for their money.** I figure I've only got one chance to make a good first impression and I do that by bulking up my offers with value-added extras. Like this:

The Million Dollar Copywriting Bootcamp
18 CD Set w/52 page workbook, plus
3 Special Bonus Reports...

- How To Write Killer Copy
- Lucky 13 Secrets of a Successful Order Form
- Magic Transitions — 97 Magic Phrases That Almost Compel Readership

I truly want people who purchase the Bootcamp to succeed. And I've thrown in everything but the kitchen sink to make sure that they do. They reward me for my generosity by buying from me again and again.

Ted knows what he's talking about. When you bend over backwards for people, they appreciate it. They begin to trust you and feel grateful to you for giving them so much for so little. That gratitude can be **leveraged to your advantage in the best, most ethical possible way.**

A satisfied customer is more likely to buy from you again and encourage other people to be your customers, too. And <u>nothing satisfies like a FREE BONUS offer</u>.

The Bonus Offer

We make buying decisions based on emotions; you've no doubt heard that statement before. However, being rational, thinking and logical humans, we also must justify our decision to buy. We do that by convincing ourselves there is enough value to justify our emotional decision.

You read a sales letter, are intrigued by the headline. Your attention is kept through the first paragraph and you decide that you want the product or service based on benefit statements you relate to.

Your prospect checks the price — and it's somewhat higher than they anticipated.

Buyers won't usually give up at this point. They will actually attempt a <u>value calculation</u> by re-looking at what they get.

That's where your bonuses can make a big difference — they either justify the cost and click your order button, or they are gone forever.

Carefully chosen, high quality, relevant bonuses can boost the perceived value of your product or service sky-high.

And everyone loves to get something for free!

Pearls & Nuggets

Sometimes, people actually <u>buy a product just because they want the bonuses being offered</u>! I've done it myself. Haven't you?

Adding Value Isn't Expensive, Especially *Perceived Value*

In case you're wondering how you'll boost profits when you're essentially "giving away the milk for free," you should consider this...

The cost of creating a "killer" bonus need not be high at all. Indeed, it can be surprisingly cheap! What matters is that it complements or supplements the value of the product or service being offered.

The key point on effectively using bonuses to enhance your online marketing business results is to

<u>stand out from the crowd in the best possible way</u> and <u>distinguish yourself as the "source" for added value.</u>

In good economic times, and especially in bad ones, everyone wants more for their money. And they'll remember kindly any business that helps them get it. I promise you that if you create a high-value bonus, you will see immediate positive results as well as long-lasting one.

Take a lazy approach to bonus and offer something that is of little interest to your customer or readily available on the Internet for free, and you'll see results, too.

Customers who never buy from you again.

The perceived value of a shoddy bonus is LESS THAN ZERO. A bonus package of hastily thrown together freebies can HURT your sales more than help them. If you can't genuinely add value to a purchase, don't try to fake it.

You won't fool anyone.

It's Bonus Time (Again and Again)

Finally, the question is: When should bonuses be mentioned in a sales process? Early and often! Let's say you're writing a sales letter...

- You could mention bonuses just under the headline to push the "self-interest" hot button of your customer

- You can mention a time-sensitive bonus on the order form to push the "I'll lose out if I don't act now" button

- Continuously add bonuses, one after another, throughout the letter until the cumulative effect is irresistible.

Whatever you do, <u>sell the *benefit* of your bonuses</u>. Remember, your offer will often stand or fall on bonuses alone.

Pearls & Nuggets

List the dollar value beside each free bonus you offer. Then be sure to refer to the total value of all the bonuses together. This adds tremendous perceived value to your offer

---

Bonuses that are different, relevant and of high perceived value will often double or even triple your sales. It's happened to me.

Now let's make it happen for *you.*

Plan of Attack – Action Steps

Here are 5 power-packed bonus ideas to increase your sales by adding tremendous value in a way that doesn't break your bank.

1. **Worksheet or Checklist —** This is a consumer favorite. It's the perfect adjunct to e-learning products. In fact, I know some people who use worksheets and checklists as **upsells** (products that complement the original sale)

If you have **a product that explains a series of steps**, processes, techniques or strategies to your customers, then pulling those into a checklist can be extremely simple and effective. Checklists are also wonderful bonuses to use for **tele-seminars**, **coaching** sessions, **consulting services, seminars** and other **educational opportunities**.

2. **Short Summary —** If you have an eBook that's hundreds of pages long, or an audio or video product that is comprehensive, you can offer a summary or condensation of your product.

Summarize the key points into 3-5 pages and you will have created a <u>high-value bonus</u> <u>without having to create additional content.</u>

3. **Audio or Video Clip —** This is the flipside of the suggestion above. If you are marketing an eBook, you can offer a related audio clip or

video that helps communicate your point, demonstrate a technique, or show an example that is related to the text.

Interviews are a great way to quickly generate high-value bonuses. A 15-20 minute telephone interview yields a 1-2 megabyte audio file that can prove very valuable to your customer base — <u>as long as it is directly related to your content.</u>

4. **Technology and Software** — If you are selling a book on Forex Trading and how to make it big in foreign exchange markets, imagine how grateful your customers would be to receive bonus software that makes it simpler and quicker to apply your techniques.

Software has a high-perceived value. And the beauty is that the Internet is rich with free or trial software that you can add to your offer at no cost.

Download.com at <u>http://www.download.com</u> is a great resource for reviews and freebies. Select "Advanced Search" link in upper right hand corner and select different License options in the drop-down list.

Another option is to <u>hire a developer</u> to create a simple software application you can offer as a bonus.

5. **Bundled Products** — This is another area where I've had a lot of personal success. You can create add-ons that increase the value of

the things you're selling. For example, Ted's <u>Million Dollar Copywriting Bootcamp</u> package is an 18-CD set that comes with a 52- page workbook and three bonus reports:

- How To Write Killer Copy
- Lucky 13 Secrets of a Successful Order Form
- Magic Transitions — 97 Magic Phrases That Almost Compel Readership

The list above should open your mind to all the different things you can do to **add value without adding expense.** Your imagination is the limit to what you can do in your own business.

So I urge you to think beyond the specific problems that your primary product or service alleviates for your customer. What ELSE can you do to make their lives better?

CHAPTER 8

TACTIC #2—TURN EVERY CALL INTO OPPORTUNITY

At a recent conference, an excited woman rushed up to me. She had called the travel supply catalog Magellan's, and when she listed the products she wanted to order, the phone rep asked her how they were going to be used. Based on her answers, he suggested other products that would better serve her needs. The shopper was delighted with his recommendations and ended up going only slightly over her budget. "I'll be a Magellan's catalog customer for life, as long as I get that personalized treatment," she told me. "It was a 'wow' experience!"

How many customers are likely to say that about you? Do you "wow" customers while increasing your company's revenue? You can...if you learn how <u>to go beyond service to sales</u>.

Many business owners' fear and resist cross selling and upselling, or proactively suggesting related or unrelated items that may increase the size or dollar amount of an order. They think it's "pushy" or "unprofessional."

These feelings get passed along to sales staffs who themselves begin to see "selling" as a negative.

But hold on a minute! Done adroitly without being pushy or seeming to force unwanted items on the customer, cross selling and upselling are extremely effective ways to **increase revenue by serving customers needs.**

That's a good thing for everyone.

Upselling

Here is the good news. The hardest sale you will ever make to a customer is the first one. With the first sale, if you deliver on your promise to the customer, you establish a mutually beneficial relationship. The customer gets what he or she wants, and you get what you want. Also, once you have received a "yes" commitment from a customer, it's easier to continue the positive pattern of continued "yeses". The customer finds it hard to break the affirmative sequence.

You then will have the opportunity to upsell them.

Pearls & Nuggets

Every time any customer contacts you by telephone, email fax, personal visit, always, always, always give him/her a chance to buy more of your products without any sales pressure whatsoever. Just the above simple, but powerful, approach has put millions of extra dollars in sales in my accounts. And billions for my clients as well. And it will put a fortune in your account too.

Done properly, everyone wins. You get a sale, of course, but your customers learn how to fix a problem that they thought couldn't be solved until you showed them the light.

Does this surprise you? It shouldn't. More often than not, **prospects don't have a clue what you're selling**. So it's your job to educate them.

There are many things you absolutely must do to maximize your success in this area including using:

Choice Questions

<u>When someone calls or visits your business, **never ask for an order.**</u> And don't pose a single question, which can be answered with a one word, "no." Why? 90% of the time it *will* be answered with that one word, and that closes the door on your dialogue.

Instead of yes-no questions, ask <u>choice questions</u> that open the door to a conversation about enhanced benefits, affordable price, and other consumer-friendly topics

- **Would you like the standard or deluxe version? (If you don't have a deluxe version, create one!)**

- **Would you like rush delivery for Tuesday or Thursday?**

- **Before we finish this order, would you like to hear about an amazing special we are running just for today?**

Always make a second offer <u>whenever anyone orders.</u> If the customer says "Thanks, but no thanks," never apply any pressure. Simply say, "Thank you for your order. We know you'll be very pleased with it. And we hope to hear from you soon. Goodbye for now."

Why Upselling Is So Profitable

Upsells are those wonderful little extras and upgrades that make a good purchase better in the consumers' eyes and more profitable in yours. Here's how....

A customer buys a $25,000 automobile, with monthly finance payments of $395. At that level of investment, the new owner will probably not object to spending an additional $2 per month for upholstery protection.

$2 a month is practically nothing to the car buyer. For the *dealer,* however, that additional sale is significant. Over 48 months it adds up to a $98 sale.

Now some would say that a $98 sale on a $25,000 vehicle is only a minimal increase in the overall sale. Why waste your time? My argument is that if it only takes 30 seconds to tack on an extra $98 to the sale.

Let's say an employee is paid $20 per hour. Do the math. The 30 seconds it takes to upsell the upholstery protection "costs" your business about 17 cents. If it only costs the company **17 cents to make $98**, that's a huge return on investment. The fact that it's attached to a $25,000 sale is completely irrelevant.

So, upselling is one of the highest and best uses of your time.

Upsells are usually small purchases that the buyer doesn't have to put a lot of thought into. The bonus is they can be extremely profitable for you as the sales person and for your organization.

Anyone can upsell. A waitress asks "Do you want fries with that?" or "Would you like your pie a la mode with ice cream?" A shoe salesperson might suggest that when you buy a pair of shoes that you also use some weatherproof spray.

3 Keys to Maximize Profits with Upselling

The best part of upselling is that it's **practically effortless**. Since it's done after the customer has decided to go ahead with a major purchase, the hard part of the sales conversation has already been done. You've already established rapport, identified needs, summarized, presented benefits, asked for the order and handled objections.

Upselling is just presenting the information in a "by-the-way" assumptive manner

- **Upselling Key #1 —Upsell Sensibly**
  Say a customer purchases an e-book from your website. Instead of trying to upsell your customer on a $3,000 seminar he/she needs to attend in person, offer a $97 tele-class that teaches the work from the e-book.

- **Upselling Key #2 — Sweeten the Deal with Sales Incentives**
Once you've made the first sale, offer a discount on the second item. Give the customer a 10% discount off their first teleclass. Sometimes a very small price break is enough to get that extra sale.

- **Upselling Key #3 — Identify Buying Patterns**
Take note of how many customers who purchase e-books also buy tele-classes. This kind of information tells you what items to pitch and when. Your grasp of market research will impress potential buyers as well.

Pearls & Nuggets

Are you familiar with the concept of "herd mentality"? It's a psychological term that explains why people tend to do what others around them are doing. As a marketer, I sometimes think of this as the "Herd Mentality". That's because when consumers learn, for example, that "90% of the people who bought this e-book also purchased the tele-seminar" it might tip them towards making that extra purchase, too. (Amazon.com uses this technique VERY successfully)

Also, make sure that you include an upsale opportunity in your autoresponder within your shopping cart. For example, someone buys an e-book. In your autoresponder, thank them for their purchase and ask them if they would like to register for the teleclass on the same subject for a discount.

The 3 Biggest Mistakes In Upselling

So if it is so easy, you might be asking, how can I go wrong? Nothing, if you avoid these mistakes:

- **Upselling Mistake #1 — No One Asks "Do You Want Fries With That?"**
  You hear it from business owners...failing business owners...all the time: "I hate to sell", "I don't want to bother people", and the ever popular "They are probably going to say no". I know this upselling business might all sound a bit contrived, but let me introduce another perspective.

Before we go further...

I'm assuming that you only provide top-notch products and services that can make your customers life easier and more enjoyable, otherwise upselling won't help you succeed. Actually, if you're selling garbage, you don't deserve to succeed.

Sorry.

So think of it this way, if you have good information or a quality product that could help people improve the their lives, you would actually be doing a *disservice* to them if you don't share the news.

- **Upselling Mistake #2 — The "Seller" Is Pushy, Rather Than Helpful**
  How can you avoid this? Being assumptive is the key. You've got to assume that the customer will naturally want your product or service. Begin the upsell with a brief benefit, and then if possible, add something unique about what you're selling.

To avoid sounding pushy, particularly if the upsell requires some elaboration, ask for the customer's permission to describe it.

- **Upselling Mistake #3 – The Upselling Lacks Heart**
  This issue really links back to the objects made in mistake number one, which is getting comfortable with selling in general. If you're embarrassed about what you're doing, that's going to come across.

On the other hand, if you truly believe in your products or service and genuinely feel that you have something of value to offer, let the buyer see your passion. If you don't...it is time to go back to the drawing board

9 Ways to Energize Your Upselling

Although upselling techniques vary greatly based on what a merchant sells, the following tips should work for you:

- **Upsell Tip #1 — Consistently Position Upsells On Web Site Product Pages**
  Look at your web pages, your printed catalog, or even your displays to find the most strategic points to place upsell offers. The critical point to bear in mind is that you want to educate the shopper.

  In other words, make sure they know where to find every related item. Also, cross-selling is about informing your customers about the depth of your selection. They already know you sell, say, DVDs. Use your cross-sell/up-sell offers to let them know you also sell DVD players.

- **Upsell Tip #2 — Capture Last Minute Sales at Checkout**
  If you can only place upsells in one spot, this is the spot to do it. For example, once a customer has placed items in his online shopping cart and goes to the check-out page to complete the sale, you can place hot products right there.

  The consumer electronics retailer Crutchfield, for example, uses its checkout page to ask customers if there's any related gear they need, like batteries or connecting wires. Clothing e-tailers will present an offer like, "you bought the pants, do you want the shirt?"

A survey done by the E-Tailing Group indicated that 38% of e-commerce sites use this tactic.

Pearls & Nuggets

It is usually best to offer a mix of price points at the check-out page. You don't want to offer a $1,000 item at the end of the sale. Also, don't forget one of the great truths of e-tailing: low-cost items make impulse purchases more likely.

Merchants use two different technologies to make these last-minute shopping cart offers: They either use a **relational database** or they make **a** generic offer. Merchants with large budgets use a database that relates past buying patterns to link the specific items a customer has in their cart with probable cross-sells.

For e-tailers that don't have an expensive database on their site, it's still effective to simply post a **best-guess generic offer** on this page.

Pearls & Nuggets

It's not a good idea to overwhelm your shopper with too many cross-sell choices. The recommendation is to limit the offers to no more than <u>three suggestions per product page.</u> Put the top three of the top ten **best-selling products** on your checkout page. Or, offer something really new, or a **product with current buzz**.

- **Upsell in Your Emails**

    While cross-sells can be included in all customer e-mails, including support and product inquiry replies, one e-mail is particularly good for these offers: **the post-order confirmation message sent out with every purchase.**

    The recipient, after all, is a customer who has already bought from you, so placing an additional product idea just a click away is a significant sales booster. Barnes & Noble, for example, sends out a list of "great deals" with its confirmation e-mails.

Clothing retailer The Gap reminds customers of its free shipping with order of $100 or more. Office supply store Staples highlights weekly specials with links back to the site

- **Upsell Tip #4 — Be Sure the Upsells Are Relevant**
Online merchants have long experimented with placing related items on each product page. They'll offer a hat next to gloves, a bracelet near a necklace. In the early days of e-commerce, almost anything might have been presented as a cross-sell, but merchants have become a lot more savvy about making relevant offers.

  Cooking.com, for example, presents a Mixmaster with extra beaters. Hewlett Packard, with its sprawling inventory, takes it several steps further, offering a complete navigational toolbar — a tab for every category — which presents a full array of related computer gear.

  If the attempted cross-sell isn't truly related to the original purchases, however, it's much less likely to produce a sale.

- **Upsell Tip #5 — Let An Expert Do Your Upsell**
This can be one of the most potent ways to pique your shoppers' interest. Present product recommendations positioned as "Our Experts Suggest" or "Our Shopping Assistant Thought You Would Like..."

  Again, relevancy is essential here. Both the wording of the offer and the offer itself must make it clear to shoppers that the expert recommendation truly relates to the purchase they're considering. Otherwise, a laundry list of expert recommendations will result in little benefit.

- **Upsell Tip #6 – Sell In Bundles**
  One of the newer trends in e-commerce is the "shop by outfit," concept, in which an entire ensemble is offered as a package deal. Most people are familiar with this idea in clothing sales, but it is also useful with make-up, furniture packages, business-in-a-box offers, etc. This takes advantage of a technique that brick and mortar stores have used for years. Seeing the whole package, the consumer thinks, "Oh, I need ALL these items".

  It is an all-inclusive approach to upselling.

- **Upsell Tip #7 — Use Promotional Offers as Enticements**
  Especially effective in promotional upselling are **limited time offers**, phrased like this: "Take advantage of this offer by the end of the week and you'll get a reduced price." Or, if a consumer buys multiple items, they get a percentage discount.

  And here's something your "inner accountant" will like: the discount doesn't have to be very high. You just need to give the customer a sense they're saving money.

- **Upsell Tip #8 — Offer Related SERVICES As Well As Products**
  Within specific categories — electronics, for example — the extended warranty is a major profit center. Yet, even a business that can't offer an extra warranty can upsell a related service.

  These related service offers might involve an in-store visit, or, the ever popular free installation of a product. Another possibility is offering related information, whether it's a free instructional manual or book, or a limited time offer of free support .

- **Upsell Tip #9 — Use the Internet to Test, Refine, and Power-Up Your Offers**
  On the Internet, changing an upsell offer may be as easy as simply changing a link on your web site. That makes testing easy. So it's in your best interest to experiment to determine which promotional offer is best...with "best" being defined as the offer that converts the most prospects.

  The key here is to **vary your price points** on offers to get a complete understanding of what price upsells work in any given season or situation. If your average price is $70, you might try upsells with items that are $35 or $50 and also a "package deal" at $95, mixing and matching the offers to see what gets response.

Pearls & Nuggets

Are your site's customers willing to opt for higher upsells in the summer? What about during the holidays? If you can, change your upsells to reflect the changing season. It makes them more immediate and more believable.

Cross-Selling

Upselling is the practice of offering customers a product in addition to the product they are currently purchasing. **Cross-selling refers to selling items that are related or can be integrated with the item being sold**.

Cross-selling is when call centers use a technique similar to the one used in inbound telemarketing, where a call center agent <u>notifies the consumer of related products or services</u> that are similar to the product or service they were originally interested in. A good example being if you have a consumer that wants to buy a PC, they may also want to purchase anti-virus software or wireless broadband.

In this case, if you continue to **remind your customers** of the additional things you sell they will be <u>encouraged to return to you in the future</u>, therefore remaining customers of yours.

Cross-selling gives you the chance to recognize customers' needs and to meet those needs with a useful product or service. Cross-selling is not selling at all; it's a valuable client service.

When done correctly, cross-selling feels like **"cross-helping."** It is the **affirmative, ongoing process of anticipating your customers' needs** so that you can maximize the services you provide and, thus, create customers for life.

For an attorney, for example, cross-selling means suggesting to every client that it's **time to draft a will.**

Cross-selling allows you to make more productive use of resources that you might otherwise waste in trying to attract prospects with whom you have no relationship. Instead, it helps you take care of people with whom you have already established some measure of trust.

One of the best ways to cross-sell is to **give a new client a tour** of your place of business. As you make the rounds, you'll have a chance to talk about your company's additional products or services and say nice things about staff and business processes.

For a bricks-and-mortar company, this has the added benefit of making your customer feel welcome and familiar with the surroundings, rather than knowing only the path from the front door to the sales desk.

Pearls & Nuggets

Cross-selling is not so much an activity as it is <u>a frame of mind</u> that allows you to look beyond solving your clients' immediate problems, to be attentive to all of their needs, and to communicate sensible and well-conceived suggestions that will help keep them out of trouble. That's **the kind of caring that cements client relationships**.

As a wise person once said: "<u>People don't care how much you know until they know how much you care.</u>"

---

6 Cross-Sells of the Online Pros

The main cross-selling techniques that have proven themselves in the online merchandising marketplace are:

- **Same product, with promotion.** This offer type works best when used in re-marketing to individuals who abandoned your web site. Try using it in emails you send to product abandoners

- **Similar product**. This offer type works best in email re-marketing efforts, and on product detail pages. For example, if someone views a v-neck red wool sweater, try offering them a turtleneck red wool sweater

- **Competing product.** This offer type works best on product detail pages. For example, if someone views a brand name product, try offering them the same product in a different brand

- **Complementary item.** This offer type works best in the shopping cart and order status pages, and in the call center. For example, if someone views a High Definition TV, try offering them a DVD player with 1080 up-conversion

- **Accessory item.** Like complementary items, accessories work best in the shopping cart and order status pages, and in the call center. For example, if someone views an inflatable raft, try offering them an air pump

- **Discovery product.** Discovery products work best on product detail pages. Discovery items are non-intuitive, data-driven offers. For example, visitors viewing the latest, trendiest items might also purchase other trendy products, even if they are unrelated to the other trendy item

Front End Acquisition vs. Back End Sales

Online internet businesses are often in the business of attracting and selling to new clients. The strategies for selling to first time customers are referred to as **Front End Acquisition.**

Front End Acquisition refers to all of the marketing and communication that happens <u>before a person becomes your customer or client</u>. It starts from the point in time when you client does not even know you until his first purchase.

The methods that work for Front End Acquisition will not work with existing clients or Back End. And the methods used to market successfully to your Back End will not work on your Front End Acquisition.

In online sales the difference in the two strategies is very distinct. A simple way of stating it would be:

- **Front End Acquisition often relies on Landing Pages** to sell to new customers
- **Back End Sales will often come through email marketing and direct mail** to sell to existing customers

Why are these different sales methods used? Because marketers need to identify the state or frame of mind his readers are at in order to write the best sales message.

In a Front End Acquisition strategy, the Landing Page will typically:

- **Have a unique website address or URL**
- **Be one page long**
- **Convincing sales copy**
- **Only lead to the order page**

But what is important to note is: your Front End Acquisition strategy can be tweaked in each of its different phases to help improve your results and your profits.

It is important to set up both a Front End Acquisition and a Back End Sales strategy. The Front End Strategy is visible on most websites. The Back End may only be visible once someone has become a customer.

What exactly is a backend sale? To a profit-seeking business person, it's the road to riches. A backend sale can be more rewarding than the original sale. And it can also be much easier.

After you have sold something to somebody (the front-end sale**),** you are in an excellent position to <u>sell them something else which compliments that first purchase.</u>

Back End Sales are usually easier to get than Front End Acquisitions...and up to 12 times less expensive. When looking at the cost of acquiring new clients, most businesses see that it is much, much cheaper to focus on Back End Sales.

Pearls & Nuggets

Many marketers will **break even** or **lose money** on their initial product (**front end**) so they can build a large list of loyal customers. They understand that back-end sales are where empires are built.

I would like to illustrate the power of backend sales by giving you the following examples. Say you have a product that you will sell for $97.00. Each week you make 5 sales. In six months you will have made 130 sales for a total of $12,610.

Then you launch a second product for $149.000 for two days only. If only 20% of your customers buy your second product, you will make 26 sales for a total of $3,874.00...**in only 2 days!**

You could, of course, repeat this process as often as you like. And with results like these, you'll want to do it often.

Pearls & Nuggets

With most products it's best to send a **new offer every three months** or so, but this will vary from product to product and it's always important to do plenty of testing.

Don't have any suitable backend products to promote? That's not a problem. You can still triple sales to existing customers by promoting an **affiliate product**. You're bound to find something that goes with your product and will offer you a good percentage of the sale price.

Pearls & Nuggets

A great back-end sales strategy for ebook sellers is to **put affiliate links into the ebook, mixed in with the text.** If you can weave the links into your "words of wisdom", recommending resources at suitable points, then you create wonderful opportunities for backend sales.

An alternative to affiliate products is drop ship products. Here you offer a product produced by a company who send the product out for you when you sell it.

As with affiliate products, you don't need to worry about fulfilling the product, even if it is a physical one.

So, what are you going to do? Settle for what you're making now, or try some of the tips out above and watch your profits soar?

Let's go even higher.

Multi-Tasking—When Customer Service Sells

What drives any successful cross- or upselling training program is the philosophy of listening for service cues first, sales cues second. This is especially true of complaints and customer service calls.

Your best performers should be able to think of a related upsell or cross-sell at the very beginning of the conversation, even if the customer is upset. But the rep should take care of the customer's problem first, and then, if the rep has been appropriately caring and helpful, he or she can ease into suggesting sales often with remarkable success.

For example, at Southern California-based Russell and Miller, a business-to-business catalog that sells merchandising products such as sale banners, racks, and tagging guns, an order entry rep in one of my training programs gave an excellent example of listening to both service and sales cues and making appropriate suggestions.

The rep said that a customer called to replace a fabric steamer he used in his retail store. It was his second call, and the rep wondered why the steamer kept breaking, but didn't say anything.

She also recalled hearing him say that he needed the new steamer right away because he had a shipment of drapes coming in soon. The rep told my training group; "If I had asked him whether he was planning to use the steamer on drapes, I'd have known why he was replacing his steamer so often. What he probably needed was a heavy-duty steamer made for draperies. That would have been an upsell because that kind of steamer is more expensive than the one he was ordering. And to make sure his steamer held up this time, I'd have suggested a cleaner so that it would not clog and malfunction. Those items could have been my first upsell and first cross-sell."

The rep was absolutely right, and deserved a big round of applause — which she got from her colleagues.

Placating upset customers is one of the most challenging tasks that any phone rep faces. Add the burden of cross-selling or upselling at the same time, and the task becomes doubly difficult, if not altogether impossible to achieve. But it can be done if your reps learn to use the right words and phrases to defuse the emotions of angry customers.

As with all service, the key is to address the problem first. By doing so, the rep builds a rapport with the customer that lays the groundwork for sales.

Each of your reps will develop his or her own unique way of soothing ruffled feathers. However, there are some proven scripts and techniques for handling difficult customer service situations. Here are a few that your reps should become familiar with:

- **Let People Express Their Emotions (Even the Ugly Ones)**
  Most business owners feel so uncomfortable with customers' anger that they rush them off the phone. But a wise choice of words can empower the rep to take full responsibility for the customer's experience on every call. For instance, while the customer is blowing off steam, use empathizing phrases, such as "I can see how that happened" or "I understand what an inconvenience that must have been." Statements like these almost inevitably calm the customer down after a few minutes.

- **Don't Use Rules and Regulations to Put Up A Smoke Screen**
  Customers want your company to be easy to do business with, and will only become more infuriated if you say that the company can't fulfill a request because "it's our policy." Instead, say, "Let me check to see what I can do." This gives

you time to judge the caller's level of irritation and salvage the customer

- **The Customer Is Always Right (Even If They're Wrong)**
Tell a customer that he or she is wrong or unfair, even if this is the truth, and you will lose the customer...even if you ultimately give the customer everything that was requested. If you cause customers to lose their dignity, they will always feel uncomfortable about doing business with you.

- **Learn to Diffuse A Ticking Bomb**
The most effective way to do this is to place the situation in perspective and avoid inflammatory words and phrases. For instance, even if the customer says he has a "problem," you can diffuse the situation with something as simple as a word change. Instead of saying, "Please describe the problem," try "Tell me about your situation (order, delivery)." It becomes a bigger problem if you call it a problem.

Similarly, saying things like "You'll have to wait until Friday for delivery" automatically pushes the customer's button. Your customer is calling on a voluntary basis and does not "have to" do anything. "We'll get the order to you by Friday" is a softer approach.

- **Ask Open-Ended Questions (After Venting Has Ended)**
Open-ended questions cannot be answered with a "yes" or "no," so the customer will provide the details of his or her complaint. But proceed with caution. If you move to questioning and problem solving too soon, without allowing your customer to express irritation first, the questioning will be interpreted as a challenge or an interrogation. This steps up the tension several notches and lengthens the call.

Pearls & Nuggets

The most effective open-ended questions begin with, "What do you need to...?" "Tell me about..." "How can I help?" Questions should start with "what" rather than "why." Why-based questions can be seen as intimidating and may put the customer on the defensive.

Plan of Attack — Action Steps

Congratulations! You've resolved the customer's problem and are now ready to move from service to sales. Here's where your energy and enthusiasm come in. Start with the base assumption that <u>additional profits can be generated as part of every customer</u>

<u>communication,</u> so ask for additional sales on every call.

The Sale That Follows the Service

The techniques you employ and the words you use will make all the difference. If you approach this as "providing extra service" rather than "wringing every last penny from my customer," you'll have no difficulty growing your customer base and increasing profits.

Practice the following techniques to get the right balance of salesmanship and helpfulness:

1. **Take Charge.** — It is essential to guide the customer's reaction by assuming a positive ending to the conversation. For instance, instead of asking, "Would you like to hear about our specials?" try, "By the way, did you know we have our best-selling product on special this week at just $60?"

   Similarly, to ask "What other items would you like to add to your order?" is a far better tactic than to say, "You don't want to add anything else to your order, do you?"

2. **Suggest, Don't Command** — In this situation, many sales reps use words such as "must," "need," and "have to," mistakenly thinking they can bully their prospects into a sale. But command words can backfire, causing a consumer

to become defensive and *less* sales responsive, rather than more.

A better tactic is **paint positive mental pictures** as you invite a consumer to make a purchase. For example, when a rep has suggested the perfect add-on item, he or she may tell the customer, "I hope you'll think about this product. I can just imagine how much you'll be helped by..." (add the benefit **the customer might like to hear,** based on the customer's own words if possible).

3. **Focus on Benefits** — Remember that from the customer's point of view, 90% of a sale is answering "What's in it for me?" Active verbs such as "gain," "improve" and "save," along with words that express benefits, such as "'new," "free," and "proven" are likely to appeal to the customer's emotions.

The impact of these words will be greater if you combine them with any needs that the customer may have expressed earlier for example, "You'll gain a savings of 50% if you buy this new cushion, which will make your back feel much better."

4. **Speak to the Heart, Not the Head (Emotion vs. Logic)**— Ask customers how they feel, not what they think, about adding the suggested item or items to their order. Asking them to think may cause them to question the appropriateness of an item, whereas asking their feelings

about it tends to help them see how it might be suitable.

5. **Always Leave The Door Open** —The last comment a customer hears is what he or she will remember. So always leave 'em smiling... and always leave 'em with a sales reminder. Rather than ending a conversation with "Have a nice day," imagine the impact if you say, "I hope we'll be able to help you again soon" especially if they were upset. *Then* say "good-bye" with a clearly warm and friendly **upward** at the end of the word.

CHAPTER 9

TACTIC #3 — CREATE NEW PRODUCTS

Once you've made a sale, you've created a thread between your business and your customer. Threads are easily broken, but you can create a connection that's as sturdy as rope if you create additional products that serve your customers' needs.

Barbara Hales, M.D.

Pearls & Nuggets

Based on the initial purchase, you already know your customer has an interest in a certain type of product or service. That means they are **pre-qualified leads** for a backend sale. Take a business that sells kittens. They know you're going to need food, litter supplies, and toys for Fluffy.

Don't Abandon Your Niche

The decision to offer new products is an exciting one, but there's one trap you need to avoid. Don't let your pursuit of profits drive you to offer random products that have nothing to do with your initial offering.

It's important to **stay in your niche**...whether you're an online business or a Hollywood star. Actors like Tom Cruise often have trouble "selling" themselves in serious roles. His movies do much better at the box office when he stays in his established niche: action hero.

Cruise played against type in the dark Eyes Wide Shut which earned just $162,091,208. Top Gun grossed $353,816,701 worldwide.

Also sweet is the M&M candy story. They understand that creating new products strengthens their core brand *and* brings in more revenue from existing customers.

First, there was Plain. Then, in 1954, M&M's Peanut was introduced. Today, you can get your M&M's any way you like them with M&M's Almond, M&M's Dark, M&M Minis, M&Ms with tie-ins to Hollywood blockbusters, and M&M's in support of good works, such as the sale of pink M&M's with a portion of the profits going to breast cancer research in the U.S.

The result of all this diversity? The estimated number of M&Ms sold each DAY in the United States alone is **two hundred million**.

You may not be selling M&M's, but you can benefit from this giant candy brand's strategy of **creating new and related products.**

Ted Nicholas says:

"This strategy has been key to my own success. It all started with

How to Form Your Own Corporation
Without A Lawyer for Under $75

Sales grew toward the million mark, and I created new products for my old customers.

- Billion Dollar Marketing Secrets
- The Million Dollar Copywriting Boot Camp

- The Millionaire Entrepreneur
- Magic Words that Bring You Riches
- How I Sold $400 Million Worth of Products and Services
- How to Publish a Book and Sell a Million Copies (my current best seller)
- The Golden Mailbox
- How to Turn Words Into Money
- Consulting Success
- Magic Transitions
- Instant Headlines
- Branding Your Business
- How to Create a Success Offer

My information product empire now includes books, home-study courses, DVD's, CD's special reports, and my world-renowned mentoring program. They're all available for sale on my website www.tednicholas.com and each is a profit-generator in its own right.

The important thing is that while each name stands alone, the group as a whole is clearly a **collective library of business strategies for success-minded entrepreneurs.**

Speaking of names...

What's In a Name? (Everything!)

Product naming is a key aspect of branding. The name you ultimately choose will reflect who you are, your company's personality and vision. But more importantly, it must unforgettably <u>embody the promise of your product's main benefit</u> to your customers. It can dovetail generically with your competition, but ideally, it should stand out from the crowd.

Where to begin? The **most important** thing of all in naming any and all products that you sell:

Convey the Benefit

Widget Brand Whisper Air Conditioner
Mr. Widget's How to Toilet
Train Your Cat eBook
The Widget Better Burger Grill

A consumer always wants to know "<u>What's in it for me</u>?" Don't be coy. Answer that question with your product name. You should also

- **Avoid Tongue-Twister Names**
  There's a little part in all of us that hates to be embarrassed. When we ask for a product or talk about it with friends, we want to sound literate and not fumble over pronunciations.

  So be kind to your potential customers and avoid tongue twisters, or any name that's uses words that are unusually long or hard to pronounce.

- **Alliteration is Helpful**
  Okay, so the president of the company likes all the longer names on your list. You can make them more memorable and/or easier to pronounce by using alliteration. Consider Circuit City. Or Downtown Disney.
  Or the most famous brand in the world, Coca Cola. All four syllables, yet they roll off the tongue with surprising ease.

- **Avoid Abbreviations**
  Abbreviations lack personality and communicate very little in terms of benefit or brand character. Sure, IBM, MCI and HP have big recognition and identity, but they also spent years and millions in virtually all media to promote their image—using images of people and situations that were warm and fuzzy.

  Billionaire Bill Gates chose Microsoft over MS (which has other connotations).

If you don't have a lot of media dollars to spend on name recognition, try for a name that conveys a benefit or **describes content.** Snapple started out with a name that combined two of its original flavors: Spice N Apple. Silk—the soy-based milk brand—combines soy and milk. Benefit-oriented names include EasyOff oven cleaner, Miracle-Grow plant food, and Hearthwarmer (a fireplace insert).

When building a business there is little more important than selecting an appropriate company or product name. Names can be **descriptive or distinctive.**

The problem with **descriptive names** is that they are very difficult to legally protect. For example you could call your software Word Processing Software or Text Editor, but neither are distinguishing or unique. A competitor could enter the market and use the same name funneling your traffic and benefiting from your product reputation.

Distinctive names can be trademarked and protected. As a result many developers combine distinctive and descriptive by adding a company or brand name: Widget Brand Word Processing Software or Widget Brand Text Editor.

Distinctive doesn't mean obscure, oblique, or so confusing that a consumer won't understand what the "thing" is.

It's important that you name all the products in your profit funnel with care so that

a. It's **clear what the product is or does**

b. It's obvious that all the products in your line are **related to the initial product** that your customers purchased.

Think about *this* manual. Think about *your* reaction when you read the title...*14 Tactics to Triple Sales.* It told you everything you needed to know with just seven magic words that sell.

Don't Forget Your International Audience

Most of us have heard the story of Chevrolet introducing the Nova brand in Spanish-speaking countries. The car tanked because "nova" means "doesn't go" in Spanish.   Fiat had a similar problem with their Uno in Finland, where "uno" means garbage.

Oops.

Canadian products require labeling in both English and French, which is why on some cookie boxes, the English phrase "without preservatives" has been unintentionally translated into the French "sans preservatives," which means "without condoms" in French.

Oh dear.

Plan of Attack — Action Steps

If, like me, you are building your success selling knowledge, it's never too early to start thinking about product names. While some people wait until their information product is created before deciding upon the name, I believe it is better to **name the information product before you begin.**

These guidelines will help you create magnetic titles that **connect with your customers on an emotional level.**

- Brainstorm adjectives

- Get synonyms (http://thesaurus.reference. com/)

- Focus on the benefits (not the features)

- Make it easy to pronounce, and easy to remember

- Must be catchy enough to stop a member of your target market in their tracks (think shocking, provocative, exciting, controversial, motivational...)

- Look at the ClickBank marketplace to see the titles of best selling info products

- Consider "How to..."

- Consider a traditional title/subtitle format. (Title gets attention, subtitle explains what it's about)

Pearls & Nuggets

Try my reduction method. (It doesn't always work. But when it does it's enormously powerful.)

Write down exactly what the product is.
Condense it into 1 sentence.
Condense the sentence into a
4-word (or less) phrase

CHAPTER 10

Tactic #4 — Make Your Product a Media "Darling"

Publicity is often overlooked as a **primary marketing tool** to gain attention and interest in a product, service, or company. What a shame. Publicity can be **much less expensive than advertising and much more powerful.**

Just what is publicity?

No matter what business you are in, you can be your own publicist! If you want to act as your own PR firm, you can **produce a simple press kit**. This kit should include a "pitch" letter and a press release regarding your company, a new product, or a unique service.

Pearls & Nuggets

Unlike advertising space, you are not directly paying for publicity coverage. So <u>target every media vehicle</u> imaginable! But give primary focus to the media avenues most relevant to your customers and those that you are most likely to get a story aired on or published in.

Look for the media that your customers use and that might be interested in your story. For example, for a local service business it will be easier to get publicity in your local newspaper than in the major metro paper—and you'll reach the same people you want to, anyway.

Develop a story angle that might appeal to each media outlet. For example, if you are pitching your restaurant to a TV station, offer to demonstrate your cooking.

How you make your business newsworthy is only limited by your creativity and ingenuity. Remember, there are no boring stories, just boring approaches to interesting stories.

8 Things You Can Do NOW to Generate Free Publicity

How do you get your share of media attention? These eight strategies will put you and your business front and center with virtually no negative impact on your budget:

1. **Send news releases** about new products and services, contests, awards, open houses, speaking engagements.

2. **Write how-to articles** for newspapers, magazines, trade publications and newsletters, and offer lots of free advice. It helps establish you as an expert.

3. **Get onto the speaking circuit**. Speaking to community groups and trade associations is a wonderful way to "create the buzz" about your business. These groups are constantly looking for new speakers.

4. **Create a web site that offers free advice**, reciprocal links, articles by and about you, story ideas about your business, an electronic media kit, and a list of experts the media can contact.

5. **Start an e-zine**. A free electronic newsletter helps you sell your products and services to an international audience and costs almost nothing

compared to expensive direct mail campaigns. With permission, you can send the ezine to reporters who cover your industry.

6. **Look for photo opportunities**. Local newspapers, TV stations, trade publications and other media are always looking for interesting photos. Call the media with ideas, or submit your own photos.

7. **Give free classes and demonstrations** through adult education programs, at schools and colleges, or at your own business. Invite the media to attend.

8. **Participate in online discussion groups** and offer lots of helpful advice. Reporters lurk here, and if they're impressed with your messages, they might contact you for a story.

Meet the Press

Once you have targeted and established appointments with print and broadcast media contacts, you can **act as your own spokesperson** to pitch your own image, product, or service. You will become the focus, the center of attention, as you create an awareness of your business that will turn into sales leads.

Pearls & Nuggets

Get to know reporters. Offer yourself as someone they can call on for background, commentary and story ideas. Call and ask, "How can I help you?" You can become the go-to expert in your niche.

No matter what business you are in, there is a publicity angle that you can capitalize on! For example, let's say that you sell life insurance in a small town. How can you possibly get publicity? Well, you could offer to **write an article** for the local paper helping people determine what level of insurance coverage is appropriate for their situation.

Get a list of contacts. The appropriate editor at newspapers and magazines or the specific show producer at radio and TV shows. Mail **a one-page letter** explaining why your story will interest their audience, perhaps also including a press release, photos, or a video.

Pearls & Nuggets

You need to develop a "hook" or a compelling reason why someone should listen to your story. Media contacts must feel strongly that knowledge of your product or service would be of some value to their audience. Take time to build a cohesive "pitch" that really conveys the unique qualities and benefits of your product or service.

Follow up with a phone call—then get ready to meet the press!

Press Releases

A great deal of publicity starts with a **press release**. A press release is a newsworthy story about your business that you submit to various media — newspapers, radio, television, magazines, etc. If they are interested in your story, they may just interview you or run your press release in their publication.

Pearls & Nuggets

The general public is **more receptive to a news story than an ad**. A press release may be your key to getting your message seen and read in an environment (the press) where it will be *trusted and believed.*

Send out a press release every time <u>something new is happening</u> with your business, but do make sure it's newsworthy. Don't send out a release when you now carry a popular children's t-shirt in red.

These five press release subjects have historically been a hit with the media:

1. **The Launch of your Website**: What is unique about your site? What problem does it solve for your visitors? What are the benefits to your visitors?

2. **Adding New Services & Products**: Again, make sure it's newsworthy. Make sure to focus on the benefits and why your target audience would be interested in the new services and products.

3. **Events:** Announce your special events like public speaking engagements, open houses, seminars, a fair you are arranging, etc.

4. **Fundraisers & Donations**: If you are running a fundraiser or making a considerable donation (i.e., 5% of your sales for the month of September), write a press release about it. It will bring attention to your business and help you run an even more successful fundraiser.

5. **Major Awards & Accomplishments**: If you've been given a prestigious award, write a press release about it. Just keep in mind, a press release is not your opportunity to brag about yourself. You still need to focus on how that award shows you can help others.

Plan of Attack — Action Steps

You don't need to be a copywriter or hire one to create an effective release. While there are various press release templates available that will get the job done, effective press releases tend to share most of the same elements.

Here are **common press release components**, and a description of what they are and how they make your press release more effective.

- **Include the Release Time**

  This line graces the top of nearly every press release distributed to the media. It tells the journalist or editor receiving it when the information in the release can be made public. Most often, that line will read FOR IMMEDIATE RELEASE. If the news weren't permitted to be released until a later point in time, the release time would read EMBARGOED UNTIL with the release date listed afterwards.

- **Don't Forget Complete Contact Info**

  At a bare minimum, every press release should include the full name of the appropriate media contact person, their phone number, and their email address. A website URL should also be added, and a mailing address can be added optionally. The idea is to make it easy for journalists to contact someone related to the news story if they need additional information. Having no, or incomplete, media contact info on a press release is quite possibly the biggest press release writing mistake you can make.

- **Write a Dynamic Headline**

  The headline is like a title. It needs to convey your general news and grab the interest of the reader right away. A common error is trying to make the headline overly "cute" rather than having it tell the journalist immediately what the news is. If you can do both, great. If not, focus the headline on the news angle... just make sure you have a solid and interesting news angle to begin with.

- **Write a 50-Word Summary**

  Generally, there's no need to have both a sub-heading and a summary, so choose the best option for your press release and distribution

model. They each serve the same purpose —
to expand upon the news very generally mentioned in your headline. Many online distribution outlets require a summary to be included.

- **Include a Dateline**

The dateline will include the date the release is being distributed, as well as the hometown or nearest metropolitan area of the company or individual presenting the news to the media.

- **Include Everything in the Opening Paragraph**

The opening or lead paragraph should start on the same line as the press release's dateline, and expands upon the headline by answering the following questions briefly: who?, what?, when?, where?, and why?

- **Expand on the Details in the News Release Body**

The body of your news release expands upon the news being presented by offering supporting details, statistics, or background information. This is where you would include quotes in your press release. The body of the press release should follow the basic inverted pyramid writing style of journalism, where the most newsworthy information is offered first, with a trickle down effect through the least newsworthy supporting details.

- **Write a Boilerplate Statement**

  The boilerplate is a more general background or "about us" paragraph regarding the person, company, or organization presenting the news. The purpose of the boilerplate is simply to provide background information to journalists, giving them a better idea of who the issuing source of the news is.

- **Include a Call to Action If Appropriate**

  If you want members of the media to take any specific action, you'll mention that at the end of the press release. This is very often just a line such as "For more information about Company ABC or this particular news story, please contact (contact's Name) at (contact's phone number.)"

- ## Let Them Know It's Over

  You need to let editors and/or journalists know when your release is finished, so they don't assume that there's another page or addenda attached. There are a few different symbols you can use to close a press release, including "###" and "-30-"

If you do have a second page, you could end your first page with something like — more —, and if you have any addenda attached (such as photos), you should mention it at the end of the news release.

CHAPTER 11

TACTIC #5 — YOUR MULTI-MEDIA MARKETING STRATEGY

For a small business, every dollar is precious. Small businesses do not advertise for the sake of advertising. Instead, they want to get the most return for their investment. Your advertising campaign should translate to greater sales, more profits and healthier bottom line.

While there are a number of venues where you can promote your business, you need to ask three important questions:

- Where are my target buyers?
- What is the best medium to reach them?
- Can I afford to launch an effective campaign using this medium?

The Internet changed how we approach our businesses, but in particular it has altered how we approach advertising, mainly because consumers have <u>changed their behaviors</u>. Yet, the **objective** today is the same as it was prior to the 1990s and the Internet: **to get sales.**

Direct marketing is a way to reach that objective. Direct marketing is simply a sales method by which advertisers approach potential customers directly with products or services.

Direct marketing strategies can be unsolicited. These include telemarketing, and unsolicited mail such as catalogs, leaflets, brochures and newspaper or magazine coupons. These solicitations reach consumers without their express permission and if done poorly, are partially responsible for giving direct marketing a bad name.

Direct marketing strategies may also be **solicited.** These would include by-request mailings, opt-in lists for newsletters and ezines, or a web page that speaks directly to a prospective customer who has found it through a search engine.

I believe that solicited direct marketing is always more effective. When a consumer opts in to a mailing list, he/she is opening the door to future communications. You don't have to force your way in. They've **put out the welcome mat for you.**

Pearls & Nuggets

A direct marketing effort lives or dies on the strength of the mailing list you use.

CHAPTER 12

TACTIC #6 — LIST-BUILDING

List building is a big part of any business success. It's one of the profitable things *I* do. Think about it. You build a database of people who are interested in your niche market or your products and they have indicated that interest by opting in to your list. It's a **ready-made traffic source** that you can tap into at any time you need to generate profits. (Which is all the time, right?)

Let's say you have a 50,000 strong list. You can stop getting new visitors for the next year or two and still make a decent income selling to the customers and prospects on your list. However, if you don't have a list, you have to constantly generate new visitors just to maintain your profits.

Now, with a list, what you have is a go-to database of people with whom you can form a relationship. And over time, many of those subscribers will buy **repeatedly from you**. *Repeatedly*!

You can't get that if you don't build a list.

Before you begin, you will need to start by creating a **privacy policy**. Assure people that you won't sell their contact information to a third party. Let them know you'll protect their identity and their privacy.

This will give people a level of comfort and make them more likely to share their details.

You can find a free privacy policy generator by visiting: http://www.the-dma.org/privacy/creating.shtml

The first challenge for any business owner is simply getting a customer to **take time out of their day and give you their personal information**. Luckily, most people love being asked what they think. If you run a business that has customers or clients that are passionate about the service or product you provide, gathering feedback and mailing list data won't be difficult.

The only real challenge you will face is how to collect it.

Some websites use **post-transaction surveys** that customers can either take or skip, while most brick and mortar businesses choose the old pen and paper route.

If you have encountered difficulty in gathering consumer feedback and mailing list information, you may have to get creative. You could try running a small **contest** where people can sign up, giving their mailing address, phone number and email and winning a prize. Even people who are slightly paranoid about giving out personal information to businesses will happily do so if they can win something. If you have the capital, make the prize even bigger.

Offer a small vacation or free hotel reservations at a fine hotel or maybe a large gift certificate at a local restaurant. You will soon find that you will be buried in mountains of raw customer data.

One final tip, if you do offer a prize of some sort, make sure you publicize the winner. Not only is it a good public relations move, most people feel that these types of contests are fixed or fake in some way and that, "no one ever really wins." It will help your credibility if you attempt one of these contests again in the future.

If you don't want to offer a prize but you still want to gather as much information as you can about your customer base, try asking for input on what you do, the products you offer and how you can improve your company. Your dedicated consumers will be more than happy to fill you in on what you could do to improve things, but you won't garner nearly the number of entries you would if you offered a prize.

Once you have that information, you will need to organize it, enter it into a database of some sort and then use it to your advantage for things like new product unveilings, sales and more. Remember, all of the raw data in the world is useless if you don't use it correctly or at all.

The processing part of the job is just as important as the gathering.

Get Personal

People like to <u>do business with other people</u>, not with soul-less companies. In a Web 2.0 world where social marketing rules, success hinges on your ability to create a unique persona and individual voice that is yours and yours alone.

Creating a personal voice for your communications makes you unique in the marketplace. There's no other "you," than you. And that helps change every marketing message in every medium you use into **a personal message, not an advertisement.**

Today's consumers use a wide range of sources to find facts that inform their buying decisions. You need to maintain a presence in all of them. How aggressive you are in any given area should be determined by your market research.

If you sell a senior estate planning package and you know from your experience that your customers prefer to be contacted by phone because they don't have an Internet connection at home, you'd be foolish to put the lion's share of your marketing budget into a website.

An important step to developing your sales and marketing plan is to select the right media to send out your message. There are no hard-and-fast rules as to which media is better. The right media for one business may be wrong for another.

Determining your media mix is up to you. But let's talk together about what can go into that mix...

Email – The Marketer's New Best Friend

In the next section, you'll learn all about the tried-and-true technique of direct mail marketing using postcards, letters, catalogs, and other printed materials. Direct mail has proven itself to be many things through the years. Unfortunately, it has proven itself to be "expensive" as well as "effective."

Imagine being able to get the entire marketing bang of a full-blown sales mailer, but at a fraction of the cost. If only there were a way to "show and tell" your customers about all the wonderful problem-solving, benefit-rich things you have for sale, without having to spend so much money on printing, postage, labels, etc.

There is a way. **The road to riches is being paved with automated e-communications.**

Electronic Marketing Options

Automation is important to all businesses. The less time we have to spend doing small tasks, the more time we have to make more money or we could spend that time doing something besides working.

Putting an online business on auto-pilot isn't difficult at all and it is all done with the use of automated e-communications such as email (electronic newsletters, autoresponders, etc.). The latest technique that is the "darling" of social media marketing is e-communication using the Internet as a base: the blog.

Let's explore each of them in detail, starting with the new (blogs) before we get to the tried-and-true (emails).

Blogs and Blogging

There's no doubt about it, blogs are hot. The numbers tell the story: there are more than **39 million blogs** in existence and 75,**000 new blogs being created every day**, according to Technorati, a resource Web site with a search engine that covers the universe of blogs.

With their interactivity and their ability to position even micro-business owners as niche experts, blogs are **the "it" marketing trend.**

As you may already know, the word "blog" is a shortened version of the term "web log." It is essentially an online "diary." Blog writers ("bloggers") have something to say and this is their conduit to communicate their ideas to the universe.

Blog *readers* will embrace a blog with a unique point of view and something to say. They'll reject a self-serving, sales-oriented blog...and can bad-mouth you and your business across a broad strip of social media boards. So when it comes to the "blogosphere" (as this area of communication has come to be called), be sure to **proceed with caution.**

If you want to use the Internet to build your following, you have to be disciplined and passionate about communicating your message online.

- If you are doing this just for publicity, it will show and you'll be rejected
- If you are doing it without a purpose, it will show and you'll be rejected
- If you are not involved personally in communicating with your readers, it will show and you'll be rejected

In other words, **do it right or don't do it at all.** You must make a commitment to be the one that gets out there and writes and talks and expresses yourself, otherwise you won't get a return on your efforts.

The Difference between a Website and a Blog

A business website may be a lot like a static bill-board. It showcases information on the Internet by displaying a collection of web pages on a server. A website can be a collection of articles, news, links, information, photographs, or anything you want... including your blog.

A blog can be its own website or part of a website that includes other pages. A typical blog generally meets one or more of the following criteria:

- Editorial Content (commentary, opinions, etc.)
- Links to external sites (often seen as recommendations)
- Interaction and "dialogue" with visitors (via comments)
- Photographs of you and your activities
- Tells stories
- Usually about a specific topic, subject, or genre
- Tends to be opinionated and personal
- Could be considered "news-y" rather than "news"

Tools for Blogging

With the development of blogging programs like **WordPress,** a powerful blogging tool with massive plugins and add-ons, the line is being crossed between websites and blogs. Blogs are often referred to as **dynamic content generators** compared to the old static content websites. In the past, websites were created with static code that displayed the content and design elements to make it look pretty.

Basically, a blogging program like WordPress, or its free hosting blog service, WordPress.com, makes it simple and easy to write articles and posts on your blog and does all the work for you. All you do is just blog. The software inputs information you supply through the **blog interface** (on WordPress known as the Administration Panels) into a database.

The program then sends commands to collect information and automatically publishes the blog on your site. Depending upon those commands, each page viewed on your blog may look different or have different content.

The Internet and blogs – your own and other people's – put the world at your fingertips with millions upon millions of people literally at your doorstep. That's a powerful audience for your marketing message. So what can you do to get it right?

I've got you covered...

Barbara Hales, M.D.

6 Smart Tips for Better Blogging

If you have the dedication and consistency to get your blog out there, post regularly and keep the relationships in the blogosphere going, you might see the fruits of your labor.

1- Do It the Easy Way. Don't get complicated with your blog. If you have to depend on someone to maintain it for you, make sure it's someone you can count on. The moment the blog stops being fun, the moment your interest starts dwindling because posting is complicated...that's the moment your blog starts to die.

2- Be Hard On Yourself. Make sure you have the discipline to post at least twice a week if you want to create a disciplined following. Be consistent about when you post new info. If your posting schedule is all over the place, you stop being a reliable source of information and people are going to place their attention somewhere else.

3- Don't Be A Bore. People appreciate the written word, but in general are more entertained by more dynamic content. If possible, include video or audio when you get a chance. Most blogging platforms today can easily integrate content from YouTube or any video site.

4- Be A Collaborator. You don't have to be the author of all your blog postings. Collaborate with colleagues. This is a great opportunity for cross-promotion. "You write for me and I'll write for you."

5- Tag Like Your Blog Depended On It. (It does!) Make sure to tag all your articles and entries. This will make it easier for the search engines to find you and can be used to navigate better on your own blog.

6- Unless You're A Designer, Let A Pro Do It. Even the tastiest morsels of information are hard to swallow when a Blog looks dreadful. A badly designed site has a negative impact on your credibility; it's like showing up to work unwashed, unshaven and in your old clothes. In most cases people will have a hard time getting to your mes-sage because your appearance is not consistent with it.

Unless you've got some graphic skills, use a **pro-fessionally designed template** if possible or hire somebody that knows his/her way around blog design. And if you're not comfortable with your writing skills, consider hiring a freelance copywriter to handle the task for you.

Consumers are better educated today because of the vast amounts of information available on the Internet. Not only will a blog convey information to your target demographic faster and cheaper than tra-ditional means, but when coupled with search engine benefits, brand visibility, and a value-based proposition, a blog should be an <u>essential part of your marketing platform</u>

Print magazines make money by selling advertising. The larger their circulation, the more influence they exert over people, and the demographics of their readers dictate how much money they make. Blogs are essentially the same...except **the only advertiser is you.** (Unless, of course, you get into affiliate relationships, third-party advertising, etc.)

The bottom line on blogs is this: the more traffic (circulation) you have, the type and quality of that traffic (reader demographics) and the influence you have over your audience will determine your ability **to sell your product and increase your profitability.**

There are many products out there available free online to help you get up and running:

Email Options

To a lot of people, the term "email marketing" automatically conjures images of an email intent on one thing — selling. In actual fact, there are a number of types of email communications you can use to promote your products and services, some of which are **not directly sales related**.

But don't worry, they can certainly contribute to their bottom line in other ways.

Autoresponders

No matter what kind of business you are in, there is a way that autoresponders can be used. Just set them up (with lots of marketing prompts and calls to action, of course), and forget it. Autoresponders run on autopilot.

An autoresponder can be used to **deliver sales messages to your opt-in customer list. It can be used to deliver email courses, to send reminders, and even to help you assemble an opt-in list** if you don't already possess one. There are many creative ways you can use your autoresponder to make additional sales and to build customer relationships.

All successful marketers will tell you that there are two tools that are vital to any type of online marketing - an opt-in list and an autoresponder. In actuality, most marketers will agree that you could take away all of their other marketing tools, but they would fight to the death to keep the list and the autoresponder!

Automation is important to all businesses.

Putting an online business on auto pilot isn't difficult at all and it is all done with the use of autoresponders!

Email Marketing Options

And there are even more ways to use email technology to reach your customers with the news they didn't even know they were waiting to hear:

- **Quick Announcements**

  Often called **postcard emails**, these are simple, brief announcements your clients might want to make <u>informing customers of a special offer</u>, a popular new product or quick fire sale. These types of emails are typically restricted to a single call-to-action and should be easy for the recipient to scan in a few seconds.

- **E-Newsletters**

  The primary purpose of an email newsletter is to <u>build upon the relationship</u> your client has with their own customers. Of course, this might (and should) indirectly result in an increase in sales, but the focus should be on providing relevant, useful content your subscribers might be interested in.

Often the content isn't directly related to your products either. For example, an online grocer might send a monthly newsletter featuring a few recipes, a story on the benefits of organic produce and a column with exercising tips.

- **Catalog Emails**

  A catalog based email is fairly self explanatory, being an electronic version of a print brochure listing particular products, with the primary goal to encourage customers to purchase. I often see designers label catalog emails as newsletters, and admittedly the lines can get blurry sometimes.

- **Press Releases**

  If you have a list of media contacts that have given you permission to contact them, email press releases can be a great way to attract news coverage. Of course, there are a number of services that can distribute your press releases to the media, but maintaining their own list of media contacts can be a great way for your client to send targeted, personalized press releases only to those contacts who will be interested.

Pearls & Nuggets

Everyone enjoys the feeling of being the first to know what's new, so let your press releases do double duty. Make your customers feel like they're on your A-List by sending them press releases, too.

Custom-Tailored to Your Customer

When considering which types of email to use, it's important to remember **that you don't need to take a one-size-fits-all approach**. Some clients will be much more suited to email newsletters than one-time announcements, while the reverse might apply to others.

The best thing about email is that it's so measurable. Try a newsletter for your client for a month or two and then look at the results. Mix up the topics you cover to see which garners the most interest. Try a different layout for each issue.

As long as you stick to the expectations you set for your client's subscribers, use your creativity to find what works best

In spite of spammers abusing the medium, email is still valued by users for **timely, rich and enticing news and advertising.** It is naturally the communications delivery system of choice for large and small online companies, but it is also a critical tool for offline businesses.

<u>More and more people are turning to their computers first as a resource for buying products.</u> So even an offline business must recognize that a consumer's emailbox, not the snail-mailbox is where products are being sold today.

Pearls & Nuggets

Email can be today's direct mail choice. Ignore it and you'll be left by the wayside. However, while postage and printing costs require some investment, offline marketing often is even more profitable than e-mail.

Like any other kind of marketing email marketing has one goal: to communicate clearly the benefits of purchasing a product or service. It all comes down to giving consumers the information they need to buy.

Despite the importance of these communications, many business owners treat writing e-mail as either a chore, a waste of time, or worst, a lesser form of communication. Because of this, it isn't given the same amount of care and attention as putting pen to paper.

So what if penmanship isn't seen, or that the stationery doesn't matter? So what if everything becomes left-justified or gets truncated during transmission? Doesn't this mean that **the words themselves** become even more important than ever before?

Following are the **guidelines that I follow when composing an electronic letter**:

- **Guideline #1 — Use Appropriate Salutations**

    When used well, salutations are an effective way to set the atmosphere of the letter. Think of it as a handshake, another way to greet your reader. It allows the reader to get into the right frame of mind, preparing him for your message.

Pearls & Nuggets

Nothing is more compelling that personalization and we all react with interest when we see our name.   When you include your prospect's name in the salutation, you're likely to get a much more positive response than with a generic, "Dear Friend. "   A personalized opening says, "This is just for you."

- **Guideline #2 — Make the Subject Matter Matter**

    Your e-mail's Subject Heading is one of the first things that your reader will see. Oftentimes, and especially during sorting, it's the only way you can distinguish one letter from the next. Make it count. It's as important as a headline on an ad or sales letter.

- **Guideline #3 — Keep a Dictionary Handy**

First of all, it's just good practice. Secondly, you'll be more confident when "experimenting" with new words and phrases. As long as you verify that what you're writing is spelled correctly and is used in the proper context, you'll naturally increase your wordpower and further enhance your own writing style. And this will, in turn, make your letters more enjoyable to read, and easier to understand.

- **Guideline #4 — No Matter What They Say, Smiley Faces Work**

Some call them emoticons, some call them smiley faces. And they're great when you really want to let your reader know what you're feeling, or how you'd like your reader to feel, and you just don't have the words nor the time to say so.

Pearls & Nuggets

Emotions are most appropriately used in casual e-mail, and most effective when used sparingly. I myself use them when I want to let the reader know that everything's okay, don't worry about it. Just as it's hard not to smile back when someone is smiling at you, the same goes for smiley faces. :-) (See what I mean?)

- **Guideline #5 — Spell It Out to Remove All Doubt**

There's nothing worse than a misunderstood letter. One way to avoid this is to **begin your e-mail with why you are writing** what you are writing, and how you have come to your conclusions. Then proceed with your comment.

The "New" Email – Social Marketing

It's hard to spend more than five minutes on a media website without discovering new concepts and tools for people and businesses to communicate with each other

- Facebook
- LinkedIn
- MySpace
- Feeds
- Micro-blogging
- IM's
- Twitter

Despite what pundits might say and we might want, there are no simple answers to how email marketing should embrace (or not) social networks and other Web 2.0 developments.

But there are concepts and approaches that help us find the answers for our own unique situations. For example...

The Web 2.0 email marketer doesn't produce marketing messages in the traditional sense. The new email marketers seek to **drive sales, opinion, web visits, downloads, registrations, ad views, ad sales, donations, or whatever else defines success for the organization**.

To achieve those goals, they happen to use email. So should you!

Polishing Social Networking Email

Is there anything you can do to make your current email campaign more "social" in nature? Yes!

- **Polishing Tip #1 — Use A Headshot**

  Every social networking site has a place for your picture. So does your email! Show those pearly whites right next to your signature to infuse some more personality into your email.

Pearls & Nuggets

It may seem like a minor change, because it is, but subtle changes like this (like creative personalization, geographic targeting, and other subtle tricks) can contribute to a waterfall effect when used together.

- **Polishing Tip #2 — Start A Group Your Subscribers Can Join**

Email, by nature, is a one-to-one communication tool. Social networking, on the other hand, is a <u>many-to-many communication tool,</u> which differentiates it from the conventional web and email experience and contributes to its popularity.

Would your subscribers be even more engaged with your content if they could discuss it with one another on Facebook? Would they then share it with their friends on the social networking sites they use?

Pearls & Nuggets

Having your subscribers communicate with one another may get them more interested in your content without you having to do any more work.

- **Polishing Tip #3 — Interact with Subscribers**

Just because email is one-to-one doesn't mean it has to be one way. Remember that people can always hit reply to anything you send them. Take advantage of that fact. <u>Ask for feedback.</u>

You can also use **polls and surveys** on social websites and include the results and subscriber feedback in your future messages. TV and radio programs do this sort of thing to keep you tuned during commercials.

- **Polishing Tip #4 – Be A Person, Not A Sales-Person**

You're a real person, right? Well, don't be afraid to write like it! Remember to connect and relate with your subscribers, and be approachable.

Pearls & Nuggets

It's possible to overdo it with the personal information, but too often I see email marketers underachieving on this front. On social networking sites, people are looking to connect and get to know peo-ple...with whom they *may* do business.

---

7 Sections of a Typical Email

The body of an email is divided into 7 distinct sections:

- **The Preheader**

These <u>small and subdued text blurbs at the top of emails</u> are getting more play these days.

Particularly as more folks browse their inboxes from mobile devices, this first glimpse of the main message becomes your crucial chance to grab their interest.

The preheader informs a recipient of what the email is about, how to view it with images and/or from a mobile device, and how to ensure future delivery via content teaser snippet(s), the "view with images" prompt and/or the "add to address book" prompt.

Pearls & Nuggets

Think about what text snippet you want customers to see first. Probably something a little more engaging than "If you are having trouble viewing this email with images..."

- **Header and Navigation**

    This often takes the form of a <u>colored banner</u> and encompasses anything that lies between your preheader and main message. It's the space for your company logo, and—depending on the message content—it may also include menu items that link to other pages of your site, just in case the main message doesn't quite strike the fancy of the viewer.

- **Primary Message**

  Your email's big push deserves a lot of attention from you since you're looking to earn the attention of your subscribers. A harmonious balance of headline, body copy and supporting images delivers maximum impact.

  This should include a prominent primary call-to-action (ideally in the form of a big, beautiful, "bulletproof" button!) and a link to a landing page with a cohesive look and message that will maintain enough interest to turn that click through into a conversion.

- **Table of Contents (TOC)**

  These come in handy for longer, newsletter-form emails that contain tons of content. A TOC allows customers to skip right to what interests them rather than having to scroll all the way down.

  The TOC works most effectively as a bulleted list at the top of your email that is anchor tagged to hotlink directly to content. Fitting this into your preview pane, along with your primary message and call-to-actions, will also help it gain enough attention to earn its keep.

- **Submessage(s)**

  Adding secondary and tertiary messages to your email gives you the opportunity to present another story or two. Just make sure you don't lose your viewers in a maze of information. Keep it clean with <u>visual prompts</u> like color, strong headlines, imagery and graphics. Submessages are usually organized in a siderail or layer-caked below the primary message.

- **Recovery Module**

  This is your final outpost, your last chance to capture the click through of anyone who may have sailed through your main message or sub-messages. The recovery module is often a <u>bar at the bottom of the email</u> that includes a list of links to your site, or potentially an incentive to grab your subscribers' interest before they slip back to their inboxes.

- **Footer**

  Using the same sort of subdued, "legalese" text that comprises the header, this is another place to include the **essential nuts-and-bolts** info. The unsubscribe link is tucked away here along with company contact details, "forward to friend" and customer service links.

Pearls & Nuggets

Do you think people's eyes light up when they see dollar signs in an email subject line? Think again. Many email users have **filters in place** — through an anti-spam tool, at their ISP, in their email program, or in their perceptive mind — that move anything containing "$$$" to the trash immediately.

Avoid The Spam Trap

If you want your message to be received, opened, and read, you should **avoid words and phrases in your subject line that are commonly associated with spam..** They include:

- Free (in all its incarnations: free gift, free info, free membership, free offer)

- Income from home

- Increase Sales

- Info You Requested

- Limited Time Offer

- Save Money

- Get Rich

- Wealthy

I know, I know. These are the words and phrases that excite consumers. You can use them in the body of your message all you wish. Just keep them away from the subject line.

Image Blocking — Avoid "Spam-y" Pictures

If you hang around any discussion of email design and production, the terms "image blocking" or "image suppression" will appear at regular intervals. But what do those terms mean?

How does image blocking impact email marketing? And how can you meet the challenge? Let's start with the basics:

What are blocked images?

The software (e.g. Thunderbird) or service (e.g. Yahoo! Mail or your corporate IT department) that manages your incoming email invests a lot of effort in keeping spam out of your inbox. And thank heavens for that!

A study done by Barracuda Networks (a leader in email security), based on an analysis of more than one billion daily e-mail messages sent to its more than 50,000 customers worldwide, found that

- 90-95% of all e-mail sent in 2007 was spam

- 50% of users received at least spam e-mails in their in-box each day

- 65% received 5-10 spam messages each day

- 13% were inundated with 50 or more spam e-mails daily

A full 57% of Barracuda's respondents said they **view spam e-mail as the worst form of junk advertising.** This is close to double the number of people (31%) who cited unsolicited snail mail as "the worst" and nearly five times the number of people who gave thumbs down to telemarketing.

Spam is so hated, that new solutions for blocking the messages are constantly evolving. Previously, most technologies for identifying (and then deleting or rerouting) spam looked at the text of the message for clues. They were pretty good at spotting the "bad" messages this way.

Unfortunately, spammers adapted. Some started replacing some (or all) of their email's text with a small piece of code that calls up a remote image from another computer on the Internet and displays it in the email.

The "clever bit" is that this image contains text, working much like a photo of a page of words would.

Since anti-spam technologies find it more difficult to "read" words displayed as a picture, rather than typed out in an email, so-called "image spam" was initially more successful in getting unsolicited messages in front of email users.

Often, emails from anybody in the user's address book bypass the image blocking feature. The new Yahoo! Mail, for example, lets users manually activate images on any single email whose images were suppressed. It also lets users choose between 3 default suppression options:

- Display all images in email, except for those in the spam folder

- Display images only in emails from contacts or certified senders

- Block all images initially

It is not enough to email. It is not enough to blog. It is not enough to have a Facebook page. What you say, what you send, **what you communicate still has to have value**. In that sense nothing has changed since the day they printed the first newspaper.

Direct Mail Marketing

Direct *mail* marketing is a sub-set of direct marketing. It involves contacting customers via sales letters, catalogs, postcards, flyers, and other printed materials that arrive, as the name suggests, by mail.

With the explosion of the Internet coupled with the rising cost of postage, many businesses simply no longer use direct mail as part of their marketing. But direct mail has been **the sales workhorse of business for generations.**

Direct mail gives you the opportunity to talk directly to hundreds, thousands, and even millions of potential customers. A letter is like a dialogue between you and your prospective customer. It is one person talking to another.

Direct mail gives you the opportunity to make the most compelling case on how your product or service will benefit the recipient...**speaking "friend to friend."**

There are certainly **challenges in direct mail campaigns.**

- Many consumers view unsolicited direct mail as junk mail

- Direct mail is more effective as a campaign rather than a one-shot. You must have a long term, well thought out marketing plan

- Your piece is competing with the entire contents of a consumer's mailbox for attention. If you don't know what you are doing, you get overlooked in the mix of other direct mailers, bills, and letters from Aunt Fanny

- The cost of printing and postage can make direct mail an expensive proposition

- It may be difficult to obtain and maintain updated, accurate mailing lists

Despite the challenges, direct mail remains **the best advertising medium** for customizing your appeal. With improved database resources and demographics, you can effectively precisely target the prospect you are aiming at and fine-tune your message so that a sale is virtually inevitable.

Within the broad category of direct mail, there are many sub-categories of communication. The method of combination of methods you choose will be determined by

- What you're selling

- Who you're targeting

- How much money you have to spend

Sales Letters

When you're looking to build urgency... When you're looking to stir up the pot... When you're looking to get people to take action...

When you're looking to take them through the pain of what happens when they don't do things the right way ...

These are the kinds things that are best conveyed in **traditional long-form sales letter.**

The most valuable single sheet of paper in all of direct marketing is a letter. When included in your direct mail package, a good letter can create **40% to 50% more response** than sending just a brochure.

Sales letter can warm the coldest of customers, pave the way for an easy entrance to a tough-to-get-a-hold-of client, and soften the hardest entrance barriers to allow you the opportunity to make a sale.

Any arguments?

All winning sales letters speak to your prospect by **creating an image in the mind** of the reader. They set the scene by <u>appealing to a desire or need</u>, then flow smoothly into the visionary part of the sales presentation.

This visionary process **describes in detail how wonderful life will be** and how good the prospect is going to feel after the product is purchased or the service has been performed.

You message should give your prospect a **clear vision of the benefits** they will receive or take away from what you are offering. For this to happen, your winning sales letter must follow a time-tested and proven formula known by the acronym: **AIDA...** (not the opera)

- A — you must get your prospect's **Attention**

- I — give your prospect an **Interest i**n what you can do for her

- D — create a **Desire** for the benefits you're offering

- A — request some **Action** from your prospect

The primary objective of a letter is usually not to sell a product, but rather to **generate a phone call, email or postcard response.** Face it, the toughest objective for any piece of paper is to sell directly: to sell a product by soliciting an order without further contact or human intervention. It would be great to close a sale by just sending a sheet of paper, but unless your sales piece is aimed 100% from the get-go at creating a direct sale, that may not happen.

Direct sales letters must **solicit orders** or their mission fails, and so does your investment. These letters are usually longer, harder selling, and more powerfully written - designed to make a person place some hard-earned dollars in an envelope and wave to it as he places it in a box. Or to make a reluctant customer call with a credit card.

Not an easy task, and tough to do with a one-page letter, especially when the product or supplier is not a known entity.

A smooth, well-written sales letter must overcome the fears and the objections of buyers, and raise their confidence and level of trust enough to buy. To succeed, this letter must cause the reader to **defy the law of reader inertia** (bodies at rest tend to stay at rest) and take a pro-active role, pick up the phone, and initiate the call. Or contact your email address.

The same is true for call-generation letters that request the reader to call, write or email to set up an appointment. These letters, while not as hard-selling as a product pitch, still need to sell the benefits of the product and tell the reader to pick up the phone and call, or the letter's goal is not met.

Pearls & Nuggets

Try offering a valuable special report, free brochure or free booklet to entice the reader to contact you. And make it a time-limited offer to overcome procrastination.

Postcards

If your marketing activity doesn't include post-cards, you're overlooking a highly effective and very low-cost sales tool. Here are 12 of the many reasons postcards should be part of your marketing program.

1. **Postcards Work In Any Niche, for Any Business** — Postcards can produce all kinds of sales activity for all types of businesses: web site traffic for online marketers, floor traffic for retail stores, sales leads for direct marketers ...and just about any other type of sales activity a business wants.

2. **Postcard Design Is Easy** — Designing an effective postcard is not complicated. It can be as simple as printing your best small ad on a 4 x 6 card and sending it to a list of potential prospects.

3. **Postcard Printing Is Inexpensive** — You can print postcards with your own computer

for about 1 or 2 cents each ...or have them printed professionally for about 4 to 8 cents each.

4. **Postcard Postage Is Thrifty** — Unless you get into specialty sizes, it costs less to mail a postcard than a letter.

5. **Postcards Are Read More Often** — Because postcards are delivered "ready to read", almost everybody will read it — even people who usually throw out other types of direct mail without opening it.

6. **Postcards Produce Fast Results** — Because postcards are simple and easy to use — they produce results fast. You can mail postcards within a few days of deciding to use them ...and you'll start getting sales activity 2 or 3 days later.

7. **Postcards In The Mail Generate Traffic Online** — One of the most effective postcard formats simply lists a few benefits of a product or service on the card and tells the reader where they can get more information. This makes them ideal for generating traffic to a web site.

8. **Postcard Are For Keeping and Sharing** — Postcards are like small billboards — and they are easy to handle. They often get saved by recipients or passed on to others ...providing

additional exposure of your advertising message.

9. **Postcards Hit Their Targets Better —** You can accurately target your best markets by sending postcards only to mailing lists of prospects likely to be interested in what you're offering ...and who also have a history of acting on offers that interest them.

10. **Postcard Results Are Easy To Measure —** Postcards normally generate over 90% of their total response within 7 to 10 days. This enables you to quickly and accurately evaluate the results of a postcard campaign.

11. **Postcards Put YOU In Control —** You can quickly boost (or reduce) your sales activity anytime you want by simply regulating the number of postcards you mail and how often you mail them.

12. **Postcards Conceal Your Marketing from Competitors —** Most advertising uses mass media where your competitors hear or see what you are doing - and copy it. Postcard marketing is personal. Only you and your prospects are aware of what you are doing.

You can mail postcards within a few days of deciding to use them ...and you'll start **getting sales activity 2 or 3 days later.**

Need I say more in support of these direct mail wonders?

Here are 5 proven tips that will help you create powerful marketing postcards guaranteed to produce a big response.

1. **Make a Big First Impression** — People like getting postcards from friends and relatives. They don't like getting advertising mail. Make your postcard look at first glance like a handwritten message from a friend instead of like an advertising announcement. It creates a warm friendly reception for your postcard.

For example, use the same typestyle and layout you would use to send a postcard to a friend. Use a date at the top ...even if it is something like "Monday, 11:15 AM". And include a real "from" name at the bottom ...even if it's not handwritten.

2. **Get to the Point** — Postcards get delivered in a format that's ready to read. Take advantage of this by making the biggest benefit you offer the first thing the reader sees. This will make them want to read the rest of your postcard.

For example, state your biggest benefit as a headline at the top of your postcard ...or make it the first item on a bulleted list of benefits ...or highlight it in bold type if it's in the body of your postcard.

3. **Understand your purpose** — Marketing postcards are most effective when they are used to generate telephone responses, website traffic or sales leads. They are less effective for closing sales because they don't provide enough space for a detailed sales message. Therefore, you should design your message to sell the reader on seeking more information instead of trying to close sales.

For example, don't include much (if any) actual information about the product or service you are selling on your postcard. Instead, promote the major benefit (or benefits) they provide. Then persuade the reader to call, visit your website or to take some other action to get more information from a source where you can close sales.

4. **Be Clear and Direct** — You have only a few seconds to get the reader's attention and to persuade them to take the action you want. Always end your postcard by telling the reader exactly what to do to get more details — and include a reason to do it immediately. Keep your message brief and make sure the reader can clearly understand it with just a quick glance.

For example, limit your postcard to just a few short sentences with blank lines between them. Reduce several sentences to a short bulleted list to save space and reading time.

5. **Stimulate Fast Action** — Just telling your reader how to get more information is not enough. You have to give them a reason to respond NOW, otherwise many will put your postcard aside to do later ...then get involved with other things and forget it.

Another highly motivational reason to "respond now" is the promise of an incentive such as a discounted price, a special bonus or some other benefit such as a valuable free report if they reply to your postcard by a deadline.

Catalogs

A recent survey by the The Response Center, an independent market research firm, found that distributors attribute **49% of product sales** to catalogs.

I'm surprised at how often product catalogs seem to be created more for artistic rather than sales purposes. They are usually designed to be as attractive or distinctive as possible, but often end up having a limited impact on the sales cycle itself.

To break that cycle, you need to thoroughly consider these questions:

• What is the purpose of this literature?

• How can I make it relevant to my prospect?

- What action do I want the prospect to take?

This last question is of course critical. Unless you spell out exactly what you want your customer to do, you won't be able to steer them.

Flyers and Handouts

Flyers and handouts are inexpensive (no postage costs) and a highly effective way to grab attention in a very busy marketplace. Flyers are a good standby tool for marketing both online and off. And there's no need to be a genius to create a great one, either.

Here are some basic guidelines to design your own flyers.

- **Make Microsoft Word Your Designer** — Begin with a basic software program like Microsoft Word or Publisher. Open up the program, then look under "File" then "New" to see if there are already existing flyer wizards for documents or templates. If so, start there and adjust one to suit your needs

- **Color Correction**

  First take a look at your project budget. Is there room for full-color printing of hard copies to distribute? If not, don't worry. Regular black ink on colored paper produces nice looking, professional flyers. Coordinate the paper color with a theme for the month, like green paper for

St. Patrick's Day, red for Christmas or Valentine's Day, or yellow and lavender for Easter

- **Keep the Style Simple**

Don't have too many different fonts, text sizes and styles in one document. Choose no more than two complimentary fonts and sizes. For ideas on which to use, start a collection of flyers that are stuck on your door, around your mailbox and placed on your car's windshield

Search your favorite industry web sites for ideas, too, by looking at their online documents for downloading. Print them out and check to see what you like and don't like about them

- **Create Tabs**

One useful idea is this: add pull tabs to the bottom, so that if the flyer is placed on a bulletin board, passersby can pull off a tab and take the info home with them. Check the Help menu for directions. Basically you add a wide text box along the bottom portion of the flyer. Then you insert one row of columns. Click on the first column and write what you want to say – not much fits here so take care! Maybe use your URL or website address and phone number.

The text will run horizontally like normal, reading from left to right. So what you do is highlight it and click on "Format" from the top menu, then "Text Direction" do make it run vertical and fit in your tabs. Do the same for each tab.

Pearls & Nuggets

Get <u>two for the price of one</u>. When you're finished, **make print flyers** for local distribution and then turn the document into an Adobe .pdf file to **distribute online.** Upload it and include links to it in your emails and forum posts. Attach the pdf to emails when you know recipients accept attachments and can take a look, too. Reach out online and off with great looking flyers and grow your business one step further!

Selling On The "Net"

A website enables your business to remain open 24 hours a day, 365 days a year! It reaches out to prospective customers who are actually trying to reach your business. Your site will educate, inform, attract new customers and even generate revenue while you sleep.

Websites are **affordable and cost effective**. Annually your cost of having a website may be less than the cost of a one-time print ad. The information on your site can save you time and money. For example, you can save time and money by reducing the number of informational phone calls that you receive such as "What are your business hours?" and save money on printed promotional literature.

Does your competition have a website? Whether or not you *should* have one, this is a perfect opportunity for you to <u>differentiate your business</u> from your competition.

3-2-1 Contact!

Along with the sales message, your **Contact Us** page is one of the most important and crucial pages on your site to get right. Even if the rest of your site succeeds in the goals, if visitors fail to find the information they need to contact you then you will bring their shopping experience to a screeching halt.

Shoppers are often skeptical if they feel they won't be able to get a hold of a real person or are limited in their contact options. With all other areas of the site working, a bad contact us page <u>may cause someone to think twice about purchasing</u> with you altogether.

Therefore, visitors should not have to hunt to find your contact information. They must be able to find a link to your Contact Us page easily and obviously from all pages of your site.

Pearls & Nuggets

Be sure to provide **multiple options** for contacting you including; phone, fax, email, snail mail, and web form. Live support can also be valuable. While you may want to direct the options toward what is most convenient for you, not providing a contact option most convenient for your visitors can be a mistake

Yellow Page Advertising

Telephone book advertising is another way to reach your market area. It is perhaps the most ideal medium. Why? People are often ready to buy now. Plus, it allows you to place your business listing or ad in selected classifications within the book, with the theory being that when people need your product or service, they look up the classification and contact you.

Sometimes, much of the "sell" copy for a product or service may be left out of your ad content. Since they're looking through the yellow pages, the people who have looked up your classification are already in the market to buy a product like yours.

The **benefits** of Yellow Page advertising are well-established:

- One ad works all year long

- Gives your prospect a method of easily locating and contacting your business, even if they didn't initially know your name

- Can help you describe the differences between you and your competition

- You pay by the month instead of one large payment

There are some **disadvantages.**

- You must commit to an entire year of advertising

- You are immediately placed with a group of your competitors, making it easy for the prospect to comparison shop

- Some classifications are so cluttered with advertising that unless the copy is powerful, your ad can become buried and ineffective

- It is only effective when a prospect looks you up in the correct classification, assuming the prospect knows what classification to look for in the first place

The thing to be aware of when you write the ad is the other firms' ads within your classification. In other words, why should the reader select your firm over your competition? That is the crucial question — and your ad should provide the answer.

Pearls & Nuggets

Make it easy for customers to find your business by advertising in the **online yellow pages**. More customers than ever are now searching the online yellow pages to find local businesses and it's not just about getting your numbers listed in the directory, it's about getting your business and website exposure in the right places. And as with all advertising, the power of your headline is critical to success.

For Headline News...and more about putting it all together...let's move on to your Plan of Attack.

Plan of Attack — Action Steps

Regardless of the medium, ads and marketing messages share several key characteristics. Write a good sales letter and you'll have the basics for a great Yellow Pages ad. Develop an amazing postcard and it can be expanded into an online video script.

Now is the time to sit down and create the **essentials of a sales message**. Here's what you need:

- **The Headline –** A short, powerful phrase that encapsulates the key benefit the consumer will receive from using your product.

Ted Nicholas has found that **73% of the buying decision** is made at the point of the headline. It's so important, Ted has created 12 different headline types!

Here are some that will probably **work best** for you:

#1 — The Simple Headline

This headline is the most basic, but it doesn't mean it's not effective! The only thing you need to do is write your #1 benefit right up front. Tell your prospects exactly what's in it for them. Simple headlines are the easiest to write because it is just your best product benefit.

- This Amazing Secret Will Save You a Fortune on Your Taxes
- You Can Take Three Strokes Off Your Handicap in One Hour
- Lose 25 lbs in 7 Days!

#2 — The How-To Headline

This headline is frequently used to sell information products because it gets right to the point.

- How to Quickly and Easily...

- How to Avoid

- How to Conquer

- How to Improve...

#3 — The Discount Headline

This headline is exactly what it sounds like...It's an announcement of a Sales Discount. Whenever you write a discount headline you must <u>include the reason WHY</u> you are offering such an awesome deal.

- Our Buyer's Mistake Is Your Good Fortune

- Save 50% On New Salesman's Samples

- 50% Savings—We have To Make Room For New Inventory

#4 — The News Headline

The News Headline is best used for a brand new product or a revolutionary new system of doing things.

I also like it for advertising in newspapers specifically because it has a NEWS feel to it.

- Announcing New Surefire 12-Step Secret System...

- Revolutionary New Product Helps...

- Never Before seen Solution....

#5 — The "News-y" Headline

These headlines might not make the front page of the Times, but they feel news-y to the people who care about the topic:

- "Ohio Man Discovers the Secret of How to Escape the Rat Race"

- "Fishing Breakthrough Catches Too Many Fish — Banned in Some States"

- "Local Cemetery Owner Reveals How You Can Cash in on Your Own Funeral"

#6 — The Guarantee Headline

By putting your guarantee or your offer, right up front, it can often increase your response rate dramatically.

- 100% Guaranteed Way to Relieve Your Stress By 232% In 7 Days or Less or Your Money Back, No Questions Asked!

- Earn Up To $345 Daily Before Lunch or Your Money Back, No Questions Asked!

#7 — The Testimonial Headline

Testimonial are the actual words of a satisfied customer, Use them to create instant rapport and increased believability with new prospects.

- The XYZ Company Changed My Life by...

- I Was Skeptical At First, But After Just Three Weeks...

- I've Known About This For Years, I Wish I'd Acted Sooner

#8 — Question Headline

You need to ask questions of the prospects that make them want to read on in order to discover the ultimate answer. The purpose is to get the reader to quickly assess his situation or to start to think about his current condition.

Would You Like To...
Do You Know How To...
Are You Fed Up With...

#9 — The Problem/Solution Headline (Be Afraid, Be Very Afraid)

If your product or service is designed to meet your prospects' needs, then you will sometimes have to jar them out of their complacency by using fear as a motivator. Open the eyes of your prospects to their painful situation. (Remember what we said early about pain and pleasure?) Then, show them how easy it is to receive the answer they need to solve their problem(s).

- What Would Happen if Your Home Were Invaded? If You Own an ARF Security System, It Never Will

- I Never Thought This Would Happen to Me. But Because of Helping Hands Food Program, My Family and I Will Be Fine

- What Would Happen to You If You Lost Your Job Today? Let Fidelity Insurance Give You The Security You Need

Pearls & Nuggets

People refer to these types of headlines as negative headlines, but whatever you want to call them, they work. FEAR is the most powerful motivation you can use, if you use it correctly. You use it to shake your prospects out of their comfort zone and make them feel the pain of their situation. Then...you give them your answer.

Now let's get back to those **sales message essentials**...

- **The Opening**

  The opening is the first sentence or first two sentences following the salutation where you begin talking about your customer and his/her problem. Use a "what's in it for you" orientation. In other words, talk about "your lawn" not "our grass seed."

- **Offer Preview**

  After the opening, I like to make a brief reference to the offer. "...and you can discover it, (prove it, enjoy it) FREE, without obligation with the certificate enclosed." It's also helpful to **"merchandise" the offer** by referring to it at several points throughout the letter. "When you send for your free demo (free trial issue, 30-day no-risk trial, etc.) and get it up and running, you'll quickly see..."

- **Sell Copy**

  List in the benefits your reader will realize when he/she tests, previews, examines your product. Remember **you're selling the offer**, not the product. It's much easier to sell a 30-day trial or a free examination than it is to sell the product itself. You'll discuss payment terms later.

- **The Offer**

  Spell out your offer in detail. What the reader gets. If you're offering a premium, this the place to sell that bit, too. An expiration date helps make the message "urgent."

- **The Guarantee**

  The guarantee speaks not to your product, but to you as an honest and fair businessperson they can trust. "Examine it, try it, use it for a full 30 days without risk" makes your sales message an invitation, rather than a risk.

- **The Call To Action**

  Detach and complete a reply card, call a toll free number, complete a questionnaire, check a box. Tell the reader what to do RIGHT NOW because that expiration date will be here before he/she knows it.

- **The P.S.**

  Punctuate the call to action with the signature, then add a P.S. Use that important space to repeat a key benefit, or add a twist or an another idea to something you've already said. Also repeat your call to action here, in slightly different words.

CHAPTER 13

TACTIC #7 — MAKE CONTACT... FREQUENTLY!

Ted Nicholas says: "When I started out I used to communicate with customers once a quarter. I then increased to once every other month and **sales doubled**. I then (with great reluctance, I was afraid it was too often) I went to once a month.

You know what? Sales doubled again! Instead of customers feeling bothered, they loved hearing about new offers, new products etc.

Now I use all the tools available to me (and you)—

- Direct Mail
- Online Sales Letters
- Postcards
- Phone Calls
- In Person Meetings
- New Technologies

E-mailing and text messaging on mobile phones is becoming the preferred delivery system for mobile marketing. Research firm eMarketer projects that the global market for ad-supported mobile messaging will rise from $1.5 billion in 2006 to $12 billion by 2011. More texts are sent per day than pieces of mail delivered by the U.S. Postal Service."

Pearls & Nuggets

Capitalize on this burgeoning trend by using **text messaging** to send coupons, give news about sales and special offers or convey updated store information.

Communicate With Customer Base

After accumulating customer information and putting it into a database, bring that information out on a regular basis and communicate with those customers and prospects over and over again.

You'll see the value of leveraging rather quickly. When you are starting out you may have a customer base of 1,000 names. By capturing contact information and beginning to communicate with customers and prospects, in a very short amount of time you will accumulate thousands more names.

Pearls & Nuggets

Your first activity to leverage your database for increased profits and revenues is communication with your customers on a regular basis. The contact frequency should be at least once a month.

If you sell a product that is not consumable or something that a customer may not need more than once, you should be looking for other products that complement your product or service and start selling them.

You can also be contacting customers to get referrals and testimonials. Just don't forget about your customers! Otherwise, they will soon forget *you.*

Telemarketing can be a great sales builder. However, you don't need to be a telemarketing expert to make it a profitable enterprise. This isn't a sale. You can simply invite your best customers to come back and do business again. The approach could be something as simple as this:

> *"Hello, Mr. Kennedy. My name is Philip. I'm calling from the Worldwide Widget Store. We just wanted to let you know how much we appreciate you as a customer. This is advance notice about a special we are having next week". (Then describe the special.)*

Conclude by saying:

> *"We would like to invite you into the store to take advantage of it this week before we let the general public know. Again thanks for doing business with us. We hope to see you again soon. If there is anything else we might help you with, please let us know. Thank you and goodbye."*

Not really difficult, is it?

Most companies have regular billings or statements going out. A simple letter or invitation duplicating the phone approach could be sent out with the billings. There's no increase in expense, only the cost of the additional paper and the modest cost of printing.

Along with your regular account statements, you could have a special invitation for them to come back and take advantage of a special offer at your place of business during that particular time. This makes your customer feel special, too.

Pearls & Nuggets

Let's say you have a current customer base of 2,000 customers. If you send out a letter and have your staff call a certain percentage of those customers, you can get as high as a **25% to 40% response** from a letter like that. Depending on the price range of your product, this could range from a few hundred to <u>several thousand dollars of business</u>. Do this on a regular basis and you can **increase the revenue of the company from 25% to 100%.** (I thought you'd like that!)

Speaking at an Internet marketing seminar, Ted Nicholas demonstrated the power of a customer list to the attendees. He made a special email offer to his customer list during his presentation at the seminar. Seventy-two hours later when the seminar ended, he had sold almost $97,000 worth of product to his list!

There is no other asset in your business that is as powerful as your customer list

If you can't handle the expense of postage for a letter, use a post card. A postcard cuts the mailing and printing costs practically in half, your message can still be an attractively worded invitation. If you don't want to spend any money on print mailings, send an email...it's basically free!

Free Postage – When Mailings Do Double-Duty

Another way to communicate with your customer base is through thank you cards. If you prefer to not incur mailing costs, include the card in their bag or box the next time they purchase your products.

The thank you card could also contain a coupon that invites them back for a 10% discount as a tangible demonstration of your appreciation for their business.

The Right Goal to Win the Game

The goal of your communication is not to sell a specific product or service, but to offer something that is much more important — an invitation with feeling... emotion...and motivation to come back. As we discussed in a previous chapter, you will also want to make certain that your unique selling proposition is featured in each of these messages.

The best type of follow-up with your customers is via email, a personal message by direct mail, or the telephone. However, if you have a lot of customers to contact, the telephone can be very time consuming. And there's the increasingly negative response that consumers have to receiving business calls at home, considering this "home invasion" an invasion of privacy.

If you sell business-to-business, it can be challenging to reach people directly because of voice mail. You know your customers. Take a moment to weigh which contact option is best to choose. A follow-up message that doesn't connect has no meaning.

By implementing a good follow-up system you'll accomplish several things:

- Increase conversion rate
- Improve and build customer goodwill.
- Increase your average sales amount per customer.

My message to you is this: Capture, communicate (follow-up) and reward your customers on a regular basis. If you do this you'll find them coming back and spending more money with your firm than ever before. You'll identify those customers that are the most likely to do more business with you. You'll find that 20% of your customers really do generate 80% of your revenue!

Capture, Communicate, Reward

The steps are easy. Almost as easy as A-B-C, the steps to keeping and building your base of loyal customers is as easy as C-C-R:

Capture
Communicate
Reward

If you'll do these three steps on a regular and consistent basis, this one idea alone will generate 25% to 100% more revenue and net profits for your business.

You may have heard the business adage that it costs a lot less to maintain a current customer than to acquire a new one. Yet despite that wisdom, it appears that too much of most business marketing is geared towards acquiring "new blood." Many owners forget that the satisfied customers they already have, and the referrals that those customers bring, are the "life blood" of their business.

Don't make the same mistake.

Capture, communicate and reward. Do it as often as possible...as often as feasible...as often as possible. If you start to experience a decline in response to an aggressive campaign, back off a little.

Your customers will give you a sense of how frequently they like to be contacted.

Follow up customer contacts by **thanking cus-tomers for their time**. This will build goodwill and extend your relationship and give you a chance to "harvest" stories of your product or service in action. Remember that if you plan to use customer stories publicly, you *must* request permission.

Pearls & Nuggets

If they are truly delighted with your prod-ucts and services, more than 95% of your customers are likely to give you permis-sion to "quote them." If you request it, a majority will gladly give you a photo for you to include in your advertising or annual report. This is one more reason it is so important for you to "kill" your cus-tomers with quality.

Analyze and Respond

Next...and this is where the "gold" can be found... **analyze consumer input**:

- **Compile customer feedback**, good and bad. Break out input by categories relevant to your business and brand. Cull direct quotes to illus-trate points. Use this input as the basis for busi-ness changes or quantitative research.

- **Track and include feedback indicators**. Track items such as the number of email messages received per day and average response time. The aim is to identify issues quickly. Even a lack of customer response may be an important sign.

- **Add a commentary section** summarizing feedback themes. WeatherBug's weekly report includes a "What the numbers don't tell you" section.

By communicating with customers directly, you open a channel that allows you to tap into customers' feelings. If you know there's an issue with your offering, technology, customer base, or competitors, you can deal with it. The sooner you identify a problem, the more quickly you can respond to it...and **sell more to the grateful customers** who appreciates your efforts on their behalf.

Are these efforts worth the cost in time and energy? In my experience, the answer is a resounding yes. The good news is that this process generally leverages existing resources, so **incremental costs are minimal**. But to be sure, you should <u>monitor cost and benefits</u> of your ongoing, proactive customer communication program.

If the expense of the effort isn't generating a greater dollars-and-cents benefit for the business (translation: more sales and profits), then you need to re-think how you're doing things. Don't rely on guesswork. Gather facts and use what you learn to inform your efforts.

It's never the right time for an ostrich approach to your existing customers. In addition to being pre-sold on your business and therefore more likely to buy from you again, satisfied customers provide a mother lode of information to help improve your sales copy, offering, Web site, and marketing.

Plan of Attack—Action Steps

Ask your customers for input at every opportunity. Any incoming inquiry is a chance to pose sales-related questions. And whenever they answer one of those inquiries, those answers provide another opportunity for you and your business to be responsive to their needs with a new profit-generating sales idea.

- **Place a "feedback" text link in the footer on every Web site page or in the site's navigation bar**. Collect customer input at every touch point. Depending on your offering, you may want to solicit customers, visitors, or both.

- **Monitor and respond to non-customer service feedback.** Responses should be timely and go beyond automated, preformatted answers when you're confronted with non-routine requests.

- **Randomly select customers and request permission to talk with them**. To get input from visitors who aren't customers, use a pop-up window or a box on the home page. Consumer time is precious; send a personalized email or call to arrange a time to talk at the consumer's convenience. Only a small percentage of customers contacted will talk to you. Consider using a special email address for these communications.

- **Talk to customers**. Consider creating a list of questions to ask. The online travel executive found allowing customers to verbally direct the conversation where they wanted was most valuable. Ask customers for their stories about using your product.

Pearls & Nuggets

A good place to put the best, most specific, spontaneous testimonials is where a consumers' eye is bound to look: in **the right-hand column of each page of your website.**

- **Leverage customer service**. Gather additional information from and about your customers. Either talk directly with customers yourself or communicate regularly with customer service reps to learn what their experience tells them are emerging issues of importance to your buyers.

CHAPTER 14

TACTIC #8 — SPECIAL EVENTS, SPECIAL DEALS, SPECIAL SALES

Do you treat your customers like numbers? Nameless. Faceless. Interchangeable, except for the digits on their MasterCard or Visa?

If you do, you're in serious danger.

Customers, of course, are people first. So a smart marketer (and successful business owner) never loses sight of the fact that each customer like everyone else, wants to feel important. It a universal truth — we all want that feeling, and will gravitate towards those that make us feel that way.

(Hint: Having customers gravitate towards you is a *very* good thing)

Your existing customers *are* special. They're the lifeblood of your business and the source of the vast majority of your profits. It's in your best interest to make them feel special and cared for.

Not sure how? Here are some of the ways that customers want you to make them feel special...written in *their* words.

- **Please Know My Name**

   I know I may have a customer or registration number and that I might need to give that to you. But I also know that once you put that number in the system, you know my name. Use it. If I hand you my credit card, now you know my name too. Please use it...especially when you're inviting me to do something

- **Make Me Part of The "In" Crowd**

   I want to be an insider. That's why I like being invited into a membership program, preferred customers program, Frequent Flyer club, frequent buyer club or anything that provides me with discounts, special services, education or surprises. If you have this kind of club, invite me to join. If you don't have one yet, please think about starting one

- ***Acknowledge Me***

I know you are busy sometimes. I can see the line. I even understand that your system might be down, or that you have five people in the phone queue. I've been there, I work too. But when I call or come by, acknowledge that I am there and let me know you are glad I'm in the line. A smile and a hello, or a "We'll be with you shortly" will go a long way

- ***Surprise Me***

A little extra something with my order or a hand written note would be nice. Maybe an unadvertised gift or special discount "just because" or a free sample of dessert is all. It doesn't have to be a big thing, and it doesn't have to be every time. If you get a good surprise, do you want to share it with others? Me too

Things that make customers feel special, from special events to special discounts and gifts, will translate into more sales for you. Skeptical that you have to spend a little to get a little? Consider this story...

An annual **Customer Appreciation Sale** held on a weekend in December has evolved into big business for Congelton Brothers PRO Hardware, an American company based in Kentucky. Sales during the day-long event are **250% higher** than the store's average Saturday, with many customers planning big purchases for the annual sale.

People are likely to feel more in a "buying mood" when you make them feel appreciated and well-cared for. So get them in the mood with specials like

- Birthday (yours or theirs) Savings Events
- Anniversary (yours or theirs) Discounts
- Preferred Customers Party (including a 30% discount on all purchases)
- Inflation Fighter Sale
- Invitation Only Private Sales

If you're willing to think outside the box, and take a fun, creative approach, there are some great ways that you can use entertainment and "hospitality" to grab the attention of your customers, clients, or prospects, and show them a great time they won't soon forget.

Plan of Attack — Action Steps

The ROI of a well-planned customer appreciation event or special discount cannot be overstated. So don't wait until holiday time and just send a greeting card to say "thank you," put your money where your mouth is (and profits generate).

Show customers you care like this:

- For retail and sales businesses, you may decide to have an "**open house**" in which you both entertain and offer special sales or buying incentives of some kind. These are often used successfully for clothing stores, restaurants, or automobile dealerships, for example. BUT... the idea can be adapted to just about any other type of sales-related business

- For professional services, such as realtors, financial planners, and health care offices, you may choose to arrange a more formal "thank you" event to **wine and dine** both your past and current clients, as well as their friends, referrals, and other prospects. These can be held on site if your office has the space, or you can use a banquet hall or other appropriate facility. And the event itself can run the gamut from a simple cocktail hour, to a more formal dinner party

- Another approach to these types of events that can be valuable to your clients is to mix the "hospitality" with an informal "**educational seminar**" and actually offer them some valuable information. This could be estate planning or investment seminars for financial planners; tips on staying healthy for health care offices such as chiropractors; or a short seminar on refinancing for realtors or mortgage specialists, just to give a few examples

Customer appreciation and "thank you" events can be a terrific way to keep your business in the minds of customers and prospects, and even help develop deeper, more long-term personal relationships with them. No matter what kind of business you're in, this kind of specialized attention and consideration towards your customers will pay off many times over in referrals, customer loyalty, and repeat business.

CHAPTER 15

TACTIC #9 — USE PACKAGE INSERTS TO SELL MORE

Because of low response rates, insert media has historically not been the first choice of marketers. But that is changing, thanks in large part to rising postage costs that have made traditional direct mail more costly.

The concept of promotional inserts in outgoing shipments is a basic one—maximize follow-up sales by using "free" space. You're already shipping an order to the customer, so who wouldn't want to maximize that contact opportunity by promoting additional items for purchase.

Package Insert Programs (PIPs) are centered around outgoing goods that have been purchased by a consumer. For mail order, the package is mailed out and additional advertising materials are included along with the purchased items. Inserts are often pre-collated in an envelope, which is then inserted inside of the package being mailed.

PIP also works at POP (Point of Purchase). Many retailers tuck their catalogs, coupons, or other sales-related materials into the bag.

Pearls & Nuggets

Since a mail order package is anticipated and desired by the consumer who ordered it, PIPs command a fairly high advertising rate. (And that's the first step to a very high conversion rate.) So look before you leap. Ask a broker for a quotation to see if the cost fits into your budget planning.

For most merchants this means throwing in a bounce-back catalog. In 90% of cases this is merely an overrun of the most recent catalog. With the exception of new online customers who have never seen your catalog, this is usually a repeat of the catalog most recently received by your previous buyers.

Since it has been seen before, this "rerun" message is less effective than something new and fresh.

Not to ruffle any catalog's feathers, but this is the lazy marketers approach. Sure, it is easy. But how about we focus on maximizing sales from that inexpensive promotion opportunity instead of just taking what we can get?

Even the bounce-back catalog can become more hard working and deliver better results with some basic targeting and offers. Create a special offer and bounce-back catalog for new customers. If a special catalog version to use as new buyer bounce-back can be prohibitively expensive, take a regular catalog and place a wrap around it thanking new customers for their business and offering them a special deal for placing another order.

You can then do the same for repeat buyer orders. Consider putting a wrap that targets major product categories. For example, if your brand sells women's apparel, create unique wraps for outerwear and intimates. Then place the intimates-focused wrapper catalog in the box of those purchasing intimates. And outerwear in outwear buy boxes. The wraps can offer special deals in the category this buyer is most likely to have interest — the category he/she is purchasing in now.

Consider whether additional or alternative in-pack inserts make sense. Additional inserts and catalogs aren't either/or propositions. You can place additional single product or service focus inserts in outgoing order cartons in addition to a bounce-back catalog.

The additional in-pack inserts will be most effective with a single hero product or service focus and a great deal. Make sure the additional inserts stand out against any bounce-back catalog in the box as well, so your customer visually recognizes they are making a unique offer from anything in the catalog. That means different trim sizes, graphic treatments and paper stocks.

If you offer a buyer club, loyalty program or house credit card, this is a great use for the in-pack insert. Hero products can also make good use of an insert that allows you to expound on their benefits, value and offer in ways you couldn't within the context of the printed bounce-back catalog.

The moment your customer opens the box to see that wonderful item they ordered is the perfect time to get them to recommend your brand to their friends and family. Make a great "get-a-friend" offer giving both the current and new customer a special deal, a free item, free shipping or a discount.

In-pack insets offer a multitude of promotion opportunities for minimal expense. Take advantage of these options by targeting and creating variety and interest with what you place in there instead of just using the knee-jerk of the traditional untargeted bounce back catalog.

Your bottom line will thank you for it.

Plan of Attack — Action Steps

As the cost of mailing your sales information increases, so does the portion of your advertising budget dedicated to postage. In many cases, the cost of delivery is greater than the cost of your mailing piece! However if you cut back on mailing costs, of course, this translates into fewer sales contacts and less revenue for your company.

An insert program allows you to insert your brochure, sales literature, or promotional flyer into an existing package and reach your customer for a fraction of normal delivery costs.

Your sales information can be adapted for **regional or national exposure**. You won't have to hassle with mailing lists and labeling services. All you have to do is send it to your fulfillment house and they take care of it for you.

Make a list of things that you already have that can be used as promotional inserts.

CHAPTER 16

TACTIC #10 — GET CREATIVE WITH CREDIT TERMS

The days of cash-on-the-barrelhead business are long gone. The world has gone credit crazy and everyone seems to expect to buy now and pay later.

You can leverage that attitude to your advantage. Surprisingly, offering several methods of payment on your website can **increase the likelihood of a purchase**. According to a recent study reported by CyberSource, North American online businesses with four or more options for payment see an average sales conversion rate of 72%.

Payment Options

So what is the payment method of choice? According to CyberSource, 99% of online businesses offer a general-purpose payment, which includes the common credit cards like Visa, MasterCard, American Express and Discover.

Other options include:

- Gift certificates
- Recurring billing
- Electronic checks
- PayPal/other non-card
- Instant credit
- Private label card

Internet shoppers like to have a choice of payment for their new iPod, airline tickets or online dating services. With all the concerns today about identity theft, some people may not be so quick to give a credit card number online, so offering a wire transfer or billable option may ease the minds of those not willing to jump on the credit bandwagon.

If your business currently offers a good mix of acceptable payment options, you are well ahead of the mainstream! Your customers probably really like that about your website. If you only allow your customers to pay with a Visa, maybe you should consider accepting other forms of payment so you don't miss out on the business your electronic check-accepting competitors are getting.

But as important as the payment options are, it's the payment terms that are the real deal makers and breakers. The terms you offer can <u>reduce risk and overcome skepticism.</u> They may also **provide savings** and will therefore make it <u>easier for the consumer to commit to a purchase.</u>

Plan of Attack — Action Steps

Figure out which of the following consumer-friendly terms you can offer to relax a consumers' vice-like grip on their wallets.

- A winning approach that has worked very well for direct response marketers on the Internet and is working as well for infomercial advertisers is the **multi-payment approach**, for example 3 payments over 90 days. The consumer commits to the full price, but has the luxury of spreading the payment out over several months

    In addition to making it *easier* to pay for the product, this method also lets the consumer **enjoy all of the benefits immediately** with only one-third of the financial risk

- Another offer you can make is **low interest or no interest financing.** Car companies live and die on this

- A favorable payment term that captures a lot of attention is a **discount for a full upfront payment**

- Compete with the same "weapon" as Amazon. com when you add **free shipping and han-dling** to your offer

Before deciding upon a program, calculate the return on your investment. The incentive option you select will **depend upon your profit margin.**

CHAPTER 17

TACTIC #11 — PUT A CELEBRITY OR EXPERT TO WORK FOR YOU

You don't need to spend millions of dollars for Elle McPherson to say she uses and loves your product in an advertisement. Or be Coca-Cola to get your products featured on hit TV shows and in blockbuster movies. The truth is, there are many low-cost and even free ways to get your products in the hands of celebrities and endorsed by them.

The most powerful recommendations are actually **NON-paid celebrity endorsements**.

Estee Lauder would send products to celebrities she didn't know in the mail and even give them to stars she spotted on the street and later at parties as she grew more successful. Princess Grace of Monaco once said this about Estee Lauder: "I don't know her very well, but she keeps sending me all these things..."

The result? The constant practice of gifting celebrities with her homemade cosmetics is what many say caused Estee Lauder's small business to explode into a $**5 billion dollar cosmetics company.**

We're obsessed with celebrities. We want to know all about them, and **we buy products and services they promote.** That's why many of us would love to have a celebrity promoting our products and services.

Don't assume that it's out of the question. There are several ways to get celebrity endorsements inexpensively or even for free.

Different Kinds of Endorsements

Endorsements run the gamut from celebrity testimonials to a niche "expert" who is a professional in a specific field. In fact, endorsements and testimonials can be broken down into four primary types:

- **CELEBRITY ENDORSEMENTS**

These campaigns feature individuals who have achieved a certain level of public recognition because of their <u>achievements in the worlds of sport, entertainment, or some other aspect of media</u>. This type of endorsement is most often employed by major companies engaged in multi-million dollar marketing campaigns. But it can also by utilized by smaller companies engaged in local or regional business activities.

Celebrities that are typically utilized by these companies are **recognizable in the community** in which the firm does business, but they do not have as high a profile as celebrities utilized in national advertising campaigns.

The services of local athletes, media personalities, and people in the news can be secured at a much lower expense than individuals that enjoy widespread national recognition. That works for you!

- **EXPERTS ENDORSEMENTS**

This form of advertising highlights the opinions of acknowledged experts. An expert endorser must have evaluated the process using appropriate techniques, and he/she must be qualified in a relevant area.

This type of endorsement should also provide supporting evidence in the form of tests, evaluations, and/or product comparisons.

- **CONSUMER ENDORSEMENTS**

These endorsements feature actual users of the product or service being sold. Advertising utilizing customer testimonials must reflect the typical experiences of customers and the genuine feelings and findings of the consumer being highlighted.

- **CORPORATE ENDORSEMENTS**

These platinum endorsements are not easy to achieve. An endorsement from a company or organizations must reflect or support the general mission of the organization, and must often comply with strict legal standards of formal endorsement.

Different kinds of endorsements resonate with different types consumers. What would sound good to YOUR customer?

Plan of Attack — Action Steps

Once you've identified the celebrity or celebrities you'd like to work with, contact them. Celebrity databases contain contact information for celebrities, agents, managers and publicists. The most thorough one I've found is Contact Any Celebrity.

Here are several ways to get endorsements:

- **Send a Freebie**

  Do this only if you think the celebrity would enjoy your product. Include a personal letter stating how much you admire him or her and why you think your product is something the celebrity would enjoy.

  For example, you might have read an article indicating that the celebrity loves funky silver jewelry, and that's what you make.

Pearls & Nuggets

Include your address, in case the celebrity decides to send a thank-you card. You can also call the publicist and ask for feedback on the product. If the publicist says the celebrity liked it, ask whether you can use that information in your marketing materials. You can also use the thank-you card in your marketing materials. And you can use the publicist's feedback or the celebrity's thank-you note in a publicity pitch to the media touting the fact that a celebrity uses your product.

- **Carpe Diem (Seize the Day)**

When Courtney Cox's daughter Coco was crawling, Tammany Atkinson of Bee's Knees saw an interview on the Late Show with David Letterman in which Cox's husband said the couple had to carry Coco throughout their home because of their hardwood floors. Atkinson sent her some pants and two weeks later received a thank-you note. Atkinson then asked Cox if she would endorse the product, and Cox agreed.

- Ask Your Celebrity Clients to Help
  I am continually astounded by people who tell me they have celebrity clients but are afraid to ask them for endorsements. This applies to people who have bought products from you online, as well. Contact them; appeal to their graciousness by asking them to help you grow your business.

- **Offer to Barter**

  Celebrity clients interested in your products or services are often willing to barter for their endorsements. I know of a food delivery service that barters with celebrities.

- **Be Charitable**

  Most celebrities have causes they support. You can often get an endorsement by offering to make a donation in the celebrity's name in a lump sum or as a percent of sales.

CHAPTER 18

TACTIC #12 — GET WITH THE PROGRAM... THE CUSTOMER REFERRAL PROGRAM

According to Forester Research, consumers trust word of mouth from friends and family more than any other form of "advertising." Why then, do so few companies focus on encouraging customers to be advocates?

In the Web 2.0 world, the old saying, "It's who you know!" is driving sales and marketing. That makes current customers terrific resources for cultivating potential new customers.

Referrals are the backbone for many salespeople and can boost the clientele of any small business. Whether you're a one-person operation or a biz with many employees, encouraging your current clients and employees for referrals (and possibly providing incentives for them) is a smart marketing move.

One of the most persuasive and cost-effective ways to promote your company is to encourage loyal customers to act as *brand advocates* and drive new business to you. The advantages of these programs are tangible and many:

- **Increases sales from a targeted audience at a low cost**

  Many customer referral programs pay for themselves several times over annually, which makes them one of the most cost effective ways to market your products or services. With results like that, can your business afford to not have a referral program?

- **Attracts new high-value customers through ongoing dialogue with existing high-value customers**

  While it's true that many customers will refer new customers to your brand naturally, building a marketing program that promotes and rewards referrals from your *best* customers can increase new customer acquisitions several times over.

- **Gives existing customers "bragging rights"**

  Also known as the *advocacy boost,* an interesting phenomenon occurs when customers make recommendations. They not only attract new customers, but they also increase their own attachment to you, increasing their overall customer value.

- **Delivers measurable results**

  Unlike many marketing programs, you can closely and continually measure your ROI.

Never Underestimate the Power of *Just Desserts*

When asked for a favor, many of us enjoy and appreciate a pat on the back. I know I do. So consider offering a "dessert" for any successful referral a customer or employee provides. Desserts could include delicious discounts on products or services, a bonus in the paycheck, or the office favorite — a dozen chocolate donuts!

Donuts or no donuts — getting new customers through referrals only sweetens your business dealings.

any of the direct mail options (letter or post-card), a "robo-call" (pre-recorded message), or a personal call

BONUS – Referral Request Letter Template

<date>

Name
Address
City, State, Zip

Dear (customer name)

For some time now, you have been a valued cus-tomer of (name of business) and we wanted you to know we appreciate your business very much.

We know you have been pleased with our service here, and we were hoping you'd be willing to refer friends, family members, and other colleagues so we can send them information on upcoming fare dis-counts and vacation packages that will be available in the coming months.

Your time and effort in participating in this Customer Referral Program won't go unnoticed! No way! We are prepared to sweeten the deal if one of your referrals decides to use our services.

If one of your referrals does business with us any-time within the next (amount of time), we will give you a (discount, free gift, etc.)...not to mention our sincere gratitude and loyalty!

So please let us know if there's anyone you think we should add to our mailing list. A self-addressed stamped envelope is enclosed for your convenience, or you may visit our website and click on our Make a Referral button.

And, as always, if we can help *you* in any way, please give us a call.

Thank you, <name of customer> for being part of our customer family.

Sincerely,

Name
Business Owner

CHAPTER 19

TACTIC #13 — FIND CUSTOMER-FRIENDLY JOINT VENTURE (JV) OPPORTUNITIES

A joint venture is a strategic alliance where two or more people or companies agree to contribute goods, services and/or capital to a common commercial enterprise. Sounds like a partnership, doesn't it? But legally, joint ventures and partnerships are not the same thing.

The main difference between a joint venture and a partnership is that the members of a joint venture have **teamed together for a particular purpose or project**, while the members of a partnership have joined together to run a "business in common."

Each member of the joint venture **retains ownership of his or her property.** And each member of the joint venture shares only the expenses of the particular project or venture.

The key to successful joint marketing is finding partners whose products and services truly appeal to your core demographic. That means you need to find out who is selling to your target market, what products and/or services they're selling, and who your target market trusts and has good relationship with. You'll then want to contact them to cut joint venture deals by offering them complementary products and/or services.

This is a win-win proposition because it adds another profit stream to both parties. If you're a reputable company that offers high quality products/services, it should be really easy for you to find other companies to partner with.

4 Winning JV Partnerships

Here are some examples of Joint Venture deals that you can go into:

- **<u>JV Deal #1 — Cross Promotions</u>**

Ideally, products are complementary which makes it ideal to enter into a partnership. For example, you can promote computer hardware to your accounting software customers and prospects, and your JV partner can do the same by promoting your accounting software to his/her existing customers and prospects.

- **<u>JV Deal #2 — Traffic for Profits</u>**

If you've a great product but don't have a big subscriber and customer list, and website traffic, you could approach those who have a great list or a high traffic website to arrange joint venture deals. Your joint venture partners can promote your great product to their list in exchange for a percentage of profits from the resulting sales.

- **<u>JV Deal #3 — Going Halfsies</u>**

Another example is the co-development of products. You might have specialized knowledge with high demand but you lack product creation skills. You can easily approach someone who's good at creating products, such as eBooks, tapes and videos, to strike a joint venture deal. You can provide the specialized knowledge while your joint venture partner can be responsible for creating the products.

- ### <u>JV Deal #4 — Make a List</u>

  You can also enter into a list building joint venture with ezine publishers where all partners promote each other's ezine at the subscription thank you page. After someone has subscribed to your ezine, you'll redirect them to the subscription thank you page where you display your joint venture partners' ezines.

The above are just some examples of joint venture deals that you can enter into. The main draw of joint venture is that it benefits all parties; it's truly a win-win business proposition. You win, your joint venture partners win, and your customers and subscribers win.

Furthermore, it's extremely low cost and low risk, and is one of the fastest way of bringing your product to market by using other people's resources.

Do it right, and joint ventures can literally explode your online sales and profits in short order.

5 Ways Joint Ventures Spike Profits

- **They provide access to a potential customer base that would otherwise be inaccessible**. Established businesses that make good JV partners have lists of customers that would be most likely to purchase the product or service you are selling

- **The possibility of establishing a good working relationship that could turn into an ongoing and mutually profitable arrangement**

- **Credibility by association.** Associating yourself with a successful partner can help to establish credibility for you and open many doors. Your Joint Venture partners' credibility will be passed on to you simply by association

- **A Joint Venture can help you to build your own opt-in list**. The all important opt-in list is the backbone of Internet marketing. Building lists takes years but with a Joint Venture partner, you can cut the time needed in half

- **You will be guaranteed a much larger response to your new product or service than you could ever hope to generate on your own**

Words of Caution

The advantages of JV partnerships are speed, access, sharing of resources and the leveraging of underutilized resources, high profits, back end income, low or no risk opportunities and massive leverage. That's quite an upside!

On the downside, JV partnerships do present the possibility of being ripped off or disappointed by unscrupulous and unprofessional JV partners. This can hurt your reputation and/or customers and associates by associating with the wrong people, even unknowingly.

For this reason, it is critical that you consider with care each JV partnership deal that is presented to you.

3 Steps to Creating a Profitable JV Partnership

- **Step #1 Decide what you need from your joint venture partner**

  In love or in business, when you're looking for a partner, you're looking for certain key attributes. When it comes to a JV partnership, ask yourself, "What expertise or resources do they need to possess in order for me to benefit?

  If you are looking for someone to promote your membership site, it may be tempting to approach the internet marketers that own the largest mailing lists. BUT...it may be more productive to look for individuals that are experts in your niche subject, whose customer lists will be more targeted to your project even if they are not as extensive.

- **Step #2 Network to find the best joint venture partnerships**

  You can easily find prospective joint venture partners at seminars. Individuals who are willing to
  take the trouble to attend seminars to improve
  their knowledge are likely to be extremely motivated as well. In addition, there is the advantage of being able to break the ice very easily
  by discussing the speeches presented by the
  speakers, and so on.

  If you identify someone you would like to partner with, be careful about how you approach
  them. If you think they would make a good
  JV partner, the chances are many other business owners will have the same idea and they
  will get asked on a regular basis. Make sure
  you're armed with good reasons why *you* are
  the best JV partner. (Most targeted list, most
  enthusiastic buyers, most closely aligned
  product, etc.)

- **Step #3 Contact a potential partner with
your proposal**

  It would be nice to sit down across the table
  from a potential partner and negotiate a deal,
  but that's not always possible. If you can't
  arrange for a face-to-face meeting, then try for
  an ear-to-ear discussion by phone.

You need to try to build a relationship with your potential partner. If they are going to enter a project with you, and potentially promote your product to their customers, they will want to know something about you and the way you work. A lot more of your personality, sincerity, honesty, etc. will come through over the phone.

Don't give them a sales pitch. A more straightforward approach will be appreciated. And don't assume they are only interested in the amount of money they can make from your project. They may be more concerned about the quality of your membership site and their credibility with their existing customer list.

If you must send an e-mail, make it a personal one and not a standard request, or the chances are they will simply delete it.

Where to Find Good JV Partners

Simply key in your niche into the major search engines such as Google, Yahoo and MSN. What you will get is a list of **authority sites and blogs** that are obviously being read by a large number of people everyday, especially those at the very top of the search rankings. Blogs are exceptionally powerful, because passionate bloggers usually have extremely good relationships with their readers and update their blogs regularly.

If you manage to set up a joint venture partnership with these influential bloggers, their endorsement of your products will surely have a very positive impact.

Another method of finding joint venture partners online is through **forums or community groups.** Simply key in "your niche + forum", and a bunch of forums will be at your fingertips. Next, go to groups.google.com and groups.yahoo.com, and you will gain access to groups of people who are immensely involved or interested in your niche.

All you have to do next is to find out the most influential people in these forums or groups. These are usually **the ones with the most number of posts, are moderators**, or have been around for the longest period of time. If you manage to set up joint venture partnerships with just a few of them, your business will definitely improve significantly.

Plan of Attack — Action Steps

Joint Venturing is an ongoing part of business. But to get going, you can follow this 4-step Quickstart Process:

Step #1 — Get Started Now

This may sound simple to you, but I can't even count high enough to count the money people have left behind by simply not asking. Remember, you do NOT have to have a big name or reputation to approach someone on a JV. What matters most is the fit of your product or service to their list, or vice versa.

Step #2 — Approach The RIGHT Partners

One common mistake is approaching sites based on what you perceive about their reach. We all tend to think "Wow, he has a huge list; we could make a fortune." While a big list is appealing, what matters most is the fit.

So, whom DO you approach? You approach sites that "complement", but don't compete with, your product or service. Simply think through what your customer might buy next and approach those sites.

People who just bought cars often change insurance carriers. People who just bought copywriting might need an autoresponder for the messages they had created. So, if you own the autoresponder service (or you are an affiliate) you approach the copywriter.

Another great match could be weight loss and clothing (show off that new slim you!) You get the idea.

Pearls & Nuggets

Don't forget your competition. Check out who links to your competitors' web site and see if they might like to offer their clients another option.

Step #3 — Automate And Personalize

While it's smart to use software to find and approach potential JV partners, it's wise to also let your personality shine through.

If you are approaching someone with a big mailing list, you can be sure others have approached as well. Write your email in such a way to be personal, and to the point. Many times the letters you will find in software products designed for the JV market are the perfect place to start.

Step #4 — Think Win-Win

The best Joint Ventures are those where both parties win. Sure, making money is good; but great JVs are about more than just the cash. A GREAT JV is one that benefits both parties and starts a relationship that carries on to the next profitable project.

No matter what product or service you promote, you CAN find great JV partners to help you sell more in less time. And when that happens you may also create the foundation for a beautiful friendship as well.

CHAPTER 20

TACTIC #14 — LOYALTY PROGRAMS

"As a customer's relationship with the company lengthens, profits rise. And not just by a little. Companies can boost profits by almost 100-percent by retaining just 5-percent more of their customers." — Fred Reichheld, American business strategist

"Loyalty," as it's defined in practice by loyalty marketing programs, is primarily a measure of behavior—share of wallet, if you will. From the earliest days of commerce, merchants have rewarded their customers with perks—from the baker's dozen to S&H Green Stamps...hoping to increase their satisfaction and secure their loyalty.

In the modern era, customer-loyalty programs become an industry all their own.

We owe that to American Airlines (AMR).

Kick-started by the 1981 advent of American's AAdvantage program, total U.S. consumer membership in loyalty-marketing programs today is more than 1 billion strong—an average of more than four programs per adult. Nearly 90% of Americans participate in some type of rewards program, and most are enrolled in more than one.

But are loyalty programs really all they're cracked up to be? Sure, they generate incremental transactions, but what happens to loyalty when the loyalty program stops? Do these programs generate true loyalty or just behavior that looks like loyalty?

5 Things Your Loyalty Program Does for You

- Solidifies connections with your best, most profitable customers
- Makes good customers more committed and more likely to buy again
- Helps in new customer acquisition with the added potential of making them bigger and better buyers in the future
- Reconnects "lapsed" customers with a reason to shop your business "brand"
- Prevents customer defection to the competition

For small businesses with an eye on their bottom line, it will be a relief, no doubt, to learn that

The magnitude of the reward is less important than the PERCEIVED VALUE of the reward

Unlike grocery chains and big box stores, small-business owners have the autonomy to thank their patrons in many unique ways. Reward your best customers informally. If you own a restaurant, give the couple that comes in for dinner every Tuesday a free dessert every once in a while. If you own a yoga studio, offer to let your regulars try a new class for free.

Chances are you recognize your best customers already, and acknowledging this will keep them coming through your doors for years to come. Here are some ways to accomplish that goal.

6 Types of Loyalty Programs

Loyalty programs are popular with customers... sometimes. Customers like them if the rewards are generous, easy to understand, and accumulate quickly. So be sure to create yours with care. A badly conceived rewards program that consumers find difficult to use will reflect badly on your business.

Below are the 6 most successful loyalty program models and some real world applications to inspire you.

LOYALTY PROGRAM #1 — REWARD POINTS

Key Concept: Giving rewards unrelated to a company's product/service, but appropriate to your customers' demographic.

Points can be exchanged for rewards, unrelated to the brand. Use this type of program when you want your program to also serve as a new guest acquisition program and to differentiate your brand from the competition. This is especially useful if you have a limited product line and don't have unlimited options of products and services.

Restaurants and service companies use this system where their product lines are limited. Administration can be complex — it needs special equipment, cards and database systems to optimise the benefits of a program. Members will also expect to be able to track and redeem their points online.

In the Real World: American Express card users accumulate points they can then use for gifts, travel, or transfer to an airline Frequent Flyer program. A restaurant program would allow points to be used for rewards with others, e.g. the Chicago-based Lettuce Entertain You restaurant group offers a wide range of travel, wine and spa packages as rewards for members of their Frequent Diner program.

LOYALTY PROGRAM #2 — REBATES

Key Concept: Giving customers money back when they buy more.

Award a gift certificate redeemable for the next purchase, when the guest reaches a certain spending level. When you have a wide selection of products, this reward program can be used to motivate new incremental purchases. It can also be used to increased store traffic. Department stores use this method to build additional sales from existing guests.

> **In the Real World**: A simple form of this are the popular Coffee Cards — your card is stamped every time you buy a daily coffee: once you have 7 (or 10 or X) stamps, you receive one free. Very simple to administer. Clubs and casinos use this method where members and card-holders have a swipe card, and can accumulate points from their gambling expenditure and apply them to food and beverage purchases.

LOYALTY PROGRAM #3 — APPRECIATION

Key Concept: Giving customers more of a company's product/service.

When guests are asked whether they would rather have cash or a reward, they will almost always take the cash. But in giving away cash, you diminish the value of your brand. So offer a rebate when the result will be incremental visits and sales. Offer an appreciation reward of your own company's products and services in exchange for accumulated points.

The goal here is to increase guest LTV (lifetime value), not to acquire new guests. It can also be used as a device to get good guests to sample more of your other products and services. Airlines, hotels, phone companies use this to accumulate points for additional services within their own brand. Seat upgrades, free tickets, hotel stays at different locations, etc.

> **In the Real World**: At the restaurant chain CafÃ© Troppo, they had a Frequent Diner's Club that offered a free Dinner for 4 voucher once a certain level of spending was reached. This encouraged customers to spend up, and kept the rewards in-house — they could only be redeemed Monday to Thursday. They were also likely to bring guests who had not visited before.

LOYALTY PROGRAM #4 — PARTNERSHIP REWARDS

Key Concept: Rewards a guest's accumulated purchases by allowing them to choose rewards from a partnering company (whose loyal customers may, in turn, be receiving rewards from your business).

Your primary goal is to acquire new guests where you have a partnership arrangement to use the partner's extensive guest database. Airlines use this frequently when they give you points for renting cars and sleeping in hotels.

> **In the Real World:** A restaurant could offer rewards to the clients of a realtor, hairdresser or other local business, in return for that business promoting you to their customer list.

LOYALTY PROGRAM #5 — AFFINITY

Key Concept: Building a lifetime value relationship with a customer based on mutual interests and not on the use of rewards.

Once a guest climbs the loyalty ladder and reaches advocate status, your brand is firmly planted in their minds. An affinity program offers special communications, value added benefits and bonuses and recognition as a valued guest. This is used where rewards are no longer needed to cultivate a long term relationship, just as a reminder to learn more about your other products and services.

> **In the Real World:** Airline frequent flyers earn Silver or Gold status once they have earned a certain number of air miles. Nightclubs have access to special rooms and benefits for members who have reached a special level of spending or are regarded as VIP customers.

LOYALTY PROGRAM #6 — COALITION

Key Concept: Teaming up with different companies to share customer data to jointly target a customer demographic.

Although slow to take off, coalitions are very clearly the next generation of loyalty programs, extremely appropriate to the Web 2.0 world of social marketing. Coalitions, as the name implies, unite multiple marketers who together offer rewards for "points" earned by consumers through purchases of goods and services from any of the aligned businesses.

The idea behind the programs is that offering customers more opportunities to earn points and more flexibility to redeem them will increase excitement in and, well, **loyalty to the plans** – a sort-of one-stop-shopping approach to loyalty.

> **In the Real World:** With three million registered American mothers, Club Mom partners include Home Depot, Payless Shoe Source, Toys R Us, and others. Nectar (UK) is the UK's largest rewards program with participating businesses including Sainsbury's grocery stores, Barclays Bank, select BP service stations, Vodaphone stores, and others. And Anything Points let consumers earn points from eBay sellers and program partners such as FTD.com, the New York Times, American Advantage, and others, and

redeem them to pay for items on eBay where PayPal is accepted.

Pros and Cons of Loyalty Programs

If you are thinking of starting your own customer loyalty program, consider some of the advantages — and disadvantages — first:

On the pro side, a loyalty program...

- **Keeps your name in front of customers —** Think of your rewards program as free advertising. Every time your customers open their wallets and see your club card, they'll think of you

- **Encourages increased sales and return business —** Even if you go with a small-scale rewards program, regular customers will appreciate knowing that their steady purchases will pay off with a free cup of coffee or free video rental. If you decide to hand out punch cards, start new customers out with a couple of extra punches to give them an extra incentive to return

- **Increases your rate of customer re-visits and encourages business during slow periods —** For example, if you have trouble getting people in the door on Mondays, make Monday your "double punch" day

- **Can provide valuable customer demo-graphic information—**
  You can ask your patrons to fill out an application for their rewards card, building a valuable database of customer names and addresses. Your application can ask any additional questions that would be useful to your marketing research, such as how often they come to your store and what they most often purchase. Also ask for special dates such as birthdays and anniversaries, and mail them special offers when these dates approach

On the con side, a loyalty program

- **May not stand out unless the road is signif-icant. (This does NOT mean expensive) —**
  As much as customers may appreciate their eventual free drink, your business will not be the only one making such an offer

The solution: If you really want your customer reward program to stand out, up the ante. Give customers a choice once they complete a card. For example, offer that free cup of coffee or 15 percent off their entire meal.

- **May be a turn off because if customers don't like the way it works**—Because punch cards and club cards are so pervasive, for example, some customers might be sick of having their wallets stuffed full of them

The solution: You might consider keeping track of customer purchases in a computer database so they won't have to, or even filing their cards at your shop and retrieving them every time they make a purchase. This would take minimal effort on your part, and customers would appreciate the extra step to make the rewards program hassle-free for them.

- **Could backfire if the offer is too far afield of your core business—** Some small-business owners may eschew punch cards and club cards altogether, and instead opt for special sales and offers for their most loyal patrons. While this can be a great approach, you do run the risk of offending customers when you're trying to extend goodwill. For example, if you send out a Valentine's Day offer, recently divorced customers may feel alienated

The solution: Make your offers as neutral as possible. For example, invite your best customers to a "VIP only" seasonal sale, as opposed to a holiday sale.

A Promise of Privacy Encourages Loyalty

Loyalty cards could be considered invasive. Chain supermarkets have faced criticism over their loyalty cards that track customers' purchasing habits, due to the fact that they force customers to share private data in order to receive sale items. If you collect customer data, make sure that it doesn't seem as if it is more for your own benefit than theirs.

Also assure customers that their information will not be sold or shared with anyone else. And don't be surprised if some customers flat-out refuse to share personal information. Consider giving them "loyalty" privileges regardless.

Final Thoughts on Loyalty

Don't bombard customers with special offers or coupons thinking that these offers will in and of themselves build loyalty. They build loyalty, all right, but to the offer, not to your business. Consumers are understandably self-serving, so they'll just go where the coupon is best.

Think of your loyalty programs as one leg of the most important item on your "To Do" list: improve customer communication and satisfaction. This builds trust and develops long-term relationships. When customers are loyal to their relationship with a business, not the discounts offered by a business, they will buy—over and over again.

Make a list of your favorite brands. It doesn't matter if it's a beverage brand, a clothing brand, or a brand of toothpaste. When you're loyal to a brand... when you have a relationship with the company that produces the product...you're willing to pay more for it, go out of your way to acquire it, and recommend it to your friends.

And you do it all for free. It's no wonder that consumer loyalty is such a sought-after commodity.

10 Ways to Make Your Loyalty Program Irresistible

- **Make It Easy For THEM**

  Structure your program to make joining as simple as possible. For instance, let your customers sign up for your loyalty program at Website checkout. Calculate and show them the value for joining, and give an immediate discount or other tangible benefit. In addition, design the program so that all your customers – from the big spenders to the bargain hunters – can participate at some level. Everyone likes to belong to a "club," especially if membership benefits include free merchandise or valuable discounts.

- **Make It Easy for YOU**

  Don't overload your marketing department. Choose vendors who are flexible and don't offer just technical expertise but also support, so that the ball is never dropped. You want a vendor that provides the one-on-one attention of a boutique environment and the standards of a worldwide corporation. Make sure your vendor is reputable and always current with the latest industry policies. Your vendor's customer service team should be knowledgeable and experienced.

- **Make the Value REAL**

Put a lot of thought into what your customer rewards will be. Carefully consider your costs and ROI, and focus on what's valuable to your customer. Calculate exactly how much margin you can afford to share with your loyal customers on products they will find attractive. Present substantial loyalty discounts with an eye toward the lifetime value of the customer.

- **Make It PERSONAL**

It costs almost nothing to call your customers by name ("Dear Susan, Thanks for being our loyal customer!"), but it makes them feel special. It also helps create the impression that your message was expressly intended for the reader, no matter how many subscribers received it.

- **Make it TARGETED**

Turn the data you receive about your customers' interests and preferences into value for them. Not only will they feel listened to and respected, it's much more likely that they'll act on something that is specifically of interest to them. For instance, if you ask your customers for a zip code, return the favor with geographically appropriate content such as seasonal promotions or local in-store specials.

- **Make It VISIBLE**

Promote your loyalty program at every customer touch point—contact center, Website, cash register, etc. Make sure your contact center reps and everyone else with customer interaction proactively promotes the program, encouraging customers to join and making joining easy for them. Code your Website to recognize and welcome loyalty program members. Write loyalty program membership into your contact center scripts. Send a card to members for use in store and online.

- **Make It VIRAL**

People like to pass valuable and exciting opportunities on to their friends, so make it easy for your customers to get others to join your loyalty program. Then reward those customers who do. You could launch a viral e-mail campaign, for example, along the lines of "When five friends join the loyalty program, you receive a 10% discount!" Also be sure to extensively promote the reward for getting friends to join.

- **Make It PROFITABLE**

  Tie your inventory control system (if you have one) into your loyalty program. Work your unsold inventory into your customer rewards, so that you move the merchandise quickly and effectively.

- **Make It TIMELY**

  Check your history to see what inventory sells slowly or usually needs to be moved, and promote this to customers far in advance at a great rate. A hotel chain, for instance, might promote discounted rooms that are typically vacant on certain weekends to targeted loyalty program members. Early birds love the special rewards available only to those smart enough to beat the crowd.

- **Make It a PARTNERSHIP**

  Sell mini and combination packages that make it easy for customers to purchase not just your merchandise but complementary products and services too. The same hotel chain might offer loyal customers a discounted vacation package featuring the hotel plus restaurant, spa, and transportation partners. A package can be much more appealing than an a la carte product, especially if the customer receives substantial savings for buying the items as a set .

Plan of Attack — Action Steps

Use these steps to determine if a loyalty program is the right sales-maker for your business:

- **Is there some level of frequency to the purchase cycle in your business**? One rule of thumb in retail is that your customers should purchase something from you <u>at least four times per year</u> for your business to be a good fit for a loyalty program

- **Is your operation a higher-margin business?** Higher-margin businesses have an easier time creating a program because they have more freedom to offer discounts or pay for the soft benefit programs. Lower margin business can have programs, but they would need to see a higher level of customer frequency to reach the point where funding the reward makes sense

- Does your business operate through multiple locations? The more locations that you have to earn and burn loyalty program currency, the more attractive your program is to potential members. That's not to say that a single location loyalty program can't succeed, but your customers will feel inconvenienced with having to go to a specific location to earn points. In addition, in the context of single location loyalty programs, you can't distribute the program costs across multiple locations

CONCLUSION

In business, your profits are your reward for your endeavors. In fact, **profitability is the only reliable measurement of a business's success**.

Profits are the very lifeblood of a business. They fuel growth, support the owners, provide for the well being of the staff, and ultimately determine the success or failure of the business.

So how can you increase your profits? By now, you should know the answer:

Sell more to existing customers

Increased profits are achieved through a step-by-step process where marketing and customer satisfaction are at the core of the business.

It is always easier to sell products or services to your existing customers because you have developed a relationship with them when you sold your first product or service to them. You will find it far less expensive to sell to old customers as compared to selling to new customers.

Your conversion ratio will be dramatically higher with existing customers! Every time you continue selling back-end products or services to existing customers, you will be building a life-long relationship. You should continually bring out new back-end products or services to sell to existing customers. They will keep buying and buying and buying...

You get the point. Enough said.

Now it's time to get out there and do!

Best wishes for your success.